SHOE LEATHER CHRISTIANITY

by

JOHNNY HUNT

Auxano Press

Auxano
PRESS

Tigerville, South Carolina

ISBN 978-1-4954-6807-0

Published by Auxano Press
Tigerville, South Carolina
www.AuxanoPress.com

Printed by Faith Printing Company
Taylors, South Carolina
www.FaithPrintingCompany.com

DEDICATION

James serves as my favorite book in the Bible. I wish to dedicate <u>Shoe Leather Christianity</u> to my favorite friend, Dr. Jim Law, my senior associate for the past 23 years. Jim has spent most of his life service in helping me succeed as a Pastor. Jim, I love you and I'm eternally grateful for your influence in my life.

CONTENTS

ACKNOWLEDGEMENTS

No one who writes a book does so in a vacuum. That is especially true in the case of the book you hold in your hands. My family has always been the context for my entire ministry. My wife Janet has been my ministry partner and has encouraged and inspired me throughout my ministry. The book of James has taught me some of the most practical truths in the Bible. It is also true that I have learned these truths as they have been modeled by Janet Allen Hunt.

My church family, First Baptist Woodstock, is the larger family which provides support and encouragement as I grow as a pastor and minister. Much of the content of this book was derived from a series of messages preached to my beloved church family. The response and feedback of members during that series has helped me to hone my thinking on the book of James. I feel uniquely blessed to have been allowed to pastor such a responsive community.

I would also like to thank the good folks at Auxano Press for inviting me to write this book as a part of their non-disposable curriculum. The goal of Auxano Press is to provide biblically sound and reasonably priced materials to help individuals and their churches experience balanced growth. The idea behind non-disposable curriculum is that you would study this material with a small group of believers and then add it to your own Christian library.

Remember and embrace Paul's advice to Timothy— "Be diligent to present yourself approved to God as a workman who does not need to be ashamed; accurately handling the word of truth" 2 Tim. 2:15.

FOREWORD

"Christianity With Shoe Leather" will be a very helpful study for anyone serious about their faith life to the point that they regularly see evidences of *works* in their lives <u>because</u> of the sincere *faith* they possess. That was the primary lesson that James desired those Jewish believers to grasp as they were scattered among the nations. Many that day, as well as in our day, would argue that we possess our faith because we do "good works." However, James wanted to set the record straight that our lives WILL undeniably produce good works that will naturally spring forth from those who are born of the Spirit and are filled with the Spirit. It often brings into question the validity of a person's salvation that never produces the fruit of the Spirit that the Apostle Paul speaks of in Galatians 5:22-23. Simply stated, James desired for each of his readers to have a faith THAT works (a genuine faith) rather than a faith that is identified BY works (a false faith). James reiterated that overarching theme in the very first chapter when he said, "Be ye doers of the word and not hearers only, deceiving your own selves." He was saying to those followers, make sure you not only "talk the talk" but you also "walk the walk."

I know of no other individual that reflects this reality and is any more qualified to write on this subject than Dr. Johnny Hunt.

He is my Pastor, friend, mentor and example. It has been an incredible privilege for me to serve the Lord and serve him for over 23 years at the time of this writing. His leadership and example has been one that has marked me for life, especially the way he so lovingly cares and gives to others. I have learned so much from watching his "good works" that is evidence of his faith in Christ.

I pray God will grant you wisdom as you begin this study. The book of James contains valuable treasures that we all need to discover and apply.

Have fun mining for these precious treasures.

Jim Law
Executive Pastor
FBC Woodstock, GA

Enduring Life's Hard Knocks

Focal Text: James 1:1–8

I've preached through the book of James twice, filling my sermon archives with more than seventy-five different messages on this short book of five chapters. For me James remains the biblical book where, perhaps more clearly than anywhere else in God's Word, we observe Christian belief connecting to Christian behavior. In short, James teaches us that *real* faith inevitably finds itself interwoven throughout each moment of our daily routine.

Most conservative scholars consider James to be the earliest written epistle contained in the canonical New Testament. Persecution became routine for the early church. From Luke's account in Acts, the pressure on the Jerusalem church became so severe that the church scattered everywhere, leaving only the apostles behind (8:2). Through another wave of persecution, Herod claimed the life of James, the brother of John (12:2). Upon observing Jewish pleasure in halting the Christian witness, Herod arrested Peter as well, hoping to please the Jews even more (12:3). God's providence intervened, however, and Peter was supernaturally spared (12:6ff.).

Thus, James wrote to believers who weren't strangers to persecution. They knew firsthand what we could call the hard knocks of life. And James' Spirit-inspired counsel to them remains as relevant to us as it was to those whom he first addressed in the first century.

Greetings to Scattered Believers Everywhere
James 1:1

The English Bible begins with "James" who refers to himself as a "bond-servant" both of God and of the Lord Jesus Christ. The name *James* is the Greek equivalent of the Hebrew Old Testament name Jacob (Gen. 25:26) and a common name in the first century. Several men in the New Testament go by James. However, only two men appear popular enough to have written a letter without also clarifying who they were—James, the brother of John the apostle (Matt. 10:2), and James, the Lord's half brother (Matt. 13:35). And since John's brother was put to death during Herod's persecution (Acts 12:2, see above), most conservative scholars believe James the Lord's brother authored the biblical book of James.

Keep in mind that James did not believe in Jesus prior to His death (John 7:2–5). James turned to faith in Christ only after Jesus' death, burial, and resurrection. Jesus appeared to James in a postresurrection appearance (1 Cor. 15:7). Afterward James' life would never be the same. He is in the upper room with his mother, praying with the other disciples as they tarried in Jerusalem for Pentecost (Luke 24:49; Acts 1:13). Furthermore, James became a leader of the Jerusalem church, presumably chairing the Jerusalem Council (Acts 12:17; 15:13). Paul referred to him as a "pillar" in the church (Gal. 2:9) while tradition calls him "James the Just."

But from James' perspective, he was merely a "bond-servant" of His Lord. Never mentioning either his parents, his status in the church, or his privilege in meeting the resurrected Lord, James displays a model of Christian humility. He only wants to be known as a slave of Jesus Christ (the Greek term translated "bond-servant" is *doulos* which means "slave"). While born a slave of sin, James was reborn a slave of Christ. Slaves were not honored for who they were but for whom they served. Proverbs 20:6 states it well: "Most men will proclaim each his own goodness, but who can find a faithful man?" (NKJV). Christians are willing slaves of Jesus Christ. Even so, only in our bondage to Jesus may we know what true freedom is. Jesus promised us full liberty in Him (John 8:32, 36) while the apostle Paul exhorted us to guard the liberty we forever have in Christ Jesus (Gal. 5:1).

Reality of Life's Hard Knocks
James 1:2–3

James wrote to believers in 50 AD, particularly to those who had been thrown from their places of security into fierce persecution under the Roman emperor Claudius. It was, therefore, fitting that James begin his letter with an address regarding the troubles in life all believers face. Let's face it, not everyone who grows old grows up. A vast difference exists between age and maturity. James challenges us to recognize every test, trial, and tribulation, including all the accompanying sorrow and disappointment, as God-given opportunities for growth and development in the Christian life.

James begins by expressing a bold demand: "Consider it all joy, my brethren, when you encounter various trials" (1:2). Note how James uses an endearing term—*brethren*. Rather than asserting his ecclesial authority, James identifies with the recipients as family members. In addition, James employs a financial term as our first response to hardship. The term translated "consider" means "to reckon" or "to count."[1] Paul used the term in Philippians 3:7 to state that whatever his former life afforded him he "counted as loss for the sake of Christ." James is not saying trials and hardships are joyful. Instead, believers are to respond to hardship with joy. Acts reveals that the disciples were joyful they were counted worthy to suffer for Christ (Acts 5:41; cp. 1 Thess. 5:17).

James goes on to affirm the stark reality of hardships believers face in this world. Notice he says "when" we encounter trials not "if" we encounter them. The truth is, when we express joy in response to the hard knocks of life, we're expressing an *uncommon* attitude toward a *common* experience. The apostle Peter told us not to be surprised when trials come our way. He wrote: "Beloved, do not be surprised at the fiery ordeal among you, which comes upon you for your testing, as though some strange thing were happening to you" (1 Pet. 4:12). Nor are the trials we encounter of a single kind. James says the trials coming our way are "various," a word denoting multicoloredness. Hardships of every stripe come our way. James tells us to consider them all with joyful hearts.

Why? Because the "the testing of your faith produces endurance" (1:3) resulting in our spiritual maturity as disciples "lacking in nothing" (1:4). Two truths about trials become self-evident from James' words. First, trials are not to be taken as personal offenses. To be tried is not the same thing as to be tempted. We're tempted to do evil, a temptation James insists God never initiates

(1:13). Rather God targets our faith by allowing trials so that our faith may be strengthened through them. Second, God desires us to learn endurance. Thus He allows into our lives those things capable of teaching us significance. In short, trials are not turmoil we tolerate but trusts we treasure.

Reasons for Life's Hard Knocks
James 1:4

Oftentimes God allows events to take place in our lives we simply don't understand. Even so, through these events we develop patience and gain a measure of wisdom we would never experience had the trial not taken place. Peter informs us, "In this you greatly rejoice, even though now for a little while, if necessary, you have been distressed by various trials" (1 Pet. 1:6). Similarly James encourages believers to "let endurance have its perfect work" (1:4). God wants trials to run their course. Hence, we must fully cooperate with the trials God sends. The apostle Paul was so convinced trials were good for us that he boldly declared, "We . . . glory in tribulations" (Rom. 5:3, NKJV).

Trials could be likened to God's pruning shears. If our lives are to produce healthy foliage, we must periodically go through a painful pruning process. James refers to this as becoming "perfect" (1:4). By "perfect" James is not alluding to moral perfection. Instead he denotes spiritual maturity. And, if through trials we become spiritually mature, it remains no surprise that we should "count it all joy" when trials come our way (1:2).

James reveals three reasons we can be joyful during trials. First, trials purify faith. Since we cannot please God without faith (Heb. 11:6), it stands to reason our faith must be continually evaluated. For James trials are designed to test faith's authenticity, faith's genuineness. After all, our Lord instructed us about counterfeit faith (cp. Mark 4:5–6; 16–17). Hence, faith must be tried to test its truthfulness. Second, trials produce patience. One man prayed, "Lord, give me patience, but give it to me now!" I'm afraid that's how glibly many of us see the means to obtaining patience. Trials, however, are designed to give us patience. In short, we learn the art of enduring (1:3). Third, trials perfect character. Tests to our faith make us whole, "lacking in nothing." While all believers who experience severe tests are not mature believers, all mature believers have experienced severe tests to their faith. In fact, it is not too much to suggest that a believer cannot be considered mature in his or her faith unless he or she has endured painful trials. That's how significant trials are to James' exhortation.

Resources to Endure Life's Hard Knocks
James 1:5–8

God doesn't offer believers a map to calculate our bearings through the murky waters of life. Instead He gives us a guide—the Holy Spirit—to lead us as we continue to surrender to Him. In particular, James introduces the believer under trial to three crucial resources at his or her disposal.

Wisdom (v. 5a)

James reveals the first resource to believers under trial by indicating its notable absence—"if any of you lacks wisdom." The term translated "wisdom" is *sophia* and means "wisdom, skill, tact, expertise in any art."[2] The term is used often in the New Testament of God's wisdom (Rom. 11:13; 1 Cor. 1:21), Christ's wisdom (Matt. 13:54; Mark 6:2), human wisdom in spiritual things (Acts 6:10; 7:10), and spiritual wisdom in human things (2 Pet. 3:15; Rev. 13:18). James refers to the last form of wisdom (cp. 3:13, 17). The wisdom James exhorts us to possess is not merely information or knowledge but spiritual knowledge applied to life.

In summary, wisdom is the practical use of God-given knowledge. Furthermore, while education might complement wisdom, it cannot create wisdom. If we "lack" this wisdom, only God can supply it (which is why we must ask for it—see below). The term translated "lack" in the English Bible was a banking term used to describe being short of money. God will never short-change His people! Our pockets can be filled with the most abundant supply. We have no control about what life brings us. However, we do have control over how we choose to respond. Wisdom allows us to respond well to the opportunities God brings our way.

Prayer (1:5b)

If we lack wisdom in our lives, we have no real need to fret, for wisdom remains abundantly available to all who ask—"let him ask." Prayer is perhaps the most powerful yet neglected resource at the believer's disposal. Jesus displayed a similar concern toward believers, asking God to supply their lacks in life. He said: "Ask, and it will be given to you; seek, and you will find; knock, and it will be opened to you. For everyone who asks receives, and he who seeks finds, and to him who knocks it will be opened" (Matt. 7:7–8). The verb tense in "ask," "seek," and "knock" are such that Jesus is indicating for us to keep on asking and we will keep on receiving, keep on seeking and we will keep on finding, keep on knocking and doors will keep on opening. The significance prayer has in the believer's life cannot be overestimated, especially when we go through tests to our faith.

Faith (1:6–8)

God not only tells us what to ask for (wisdom), but He also tells us how to ask—*in faith*. We must believe God will answer according to His will. While we have nothing to prove by asking in faith, asking in faith pleases God (Heb. 11:6). Furthermore, asking in faith shows we have no plan B in mind. Thus, asking in faith is just the opposite of asking with "doubt" (1:6). A person plagued with doubt is likened to a ship driven by the wind on a stormy sea. It has no anchor; thus it possesses no stability. Therefore, it could easily crash on the rocky shore. In addition, a man praying without faith is likened to a man who possesses two minds on every matter. Only confusion results from a "double-minded" person. Faith is our only cure!

James thus gives us three resources to endure the hard knocks of life—wisdom, prayer, and faith. With these sources of spiritual strength, believers can walk through life counting it all joy even when they encounter various trials.

For Memory and Meditation
"Consider it all joy, my brethren, when you encounter various trials." James 1:2

[1] Spiros Zodhiates, *The Complete Word Study Dictionary: New Testament* (Chattanooga, TN: AMG Publishers, 2000).
[2] Ibid.

Real Faith

Focal Text: James 1:9–27

The story is told that during the presidency of Millard Fillmore, the cabinet was in session and trying to draw Daniel Webster, then secretary of state, into the conversation. They asked him, "What is the most important thought you ever had?"

After a moment of silence, Webster replied, "The most important thought I ever had is that, as a child of God, I am accountable to Him." If we are accountable to God, then surely we both want and need to know if our faith in God is genuine.

Biblical faith—that is, *genuine* faith—bears a number of qualities we may identify. As we walk through our passage together, these qualities will become clearly evident.

Real Faith and Humility
James 1:9–12

According to Scripture, the way up is always down in the kingdom of God. Jesus as much as said so: "Whoever exalts himself shall be humbled; and whoever humbles himself shall be exalted" (Matt. 23:12). In fact, humility characterized the Son's incarnation. In one of the most explicit passages concerning Jesus' descent to earth, Paul wrote, "Being found in appearance as a man, He humbled Himself by becoming obedient to the point of death, even death on a cross" (Phil. 2:8). Thus, James instructs the believer of "humble circumstances" to "glory in his high position" (1:9). Real

11

faith bears a striking humility. While humility could potentially exist apart from genuine faith, genuine faith always bears genuine humility. To illustrate, James compares a man of "humble circumstances" (v. 9) to a man of abundant circumstances (v. 10), the latter of which is to take note of his humiliation while the former glories in his exaltation! In short, spiritual riches are completely independent of material blessings. Spiritual riches last forever while material abundance will soon "fade away" (v. 11).

Faith that is humble trusts God to take care of the future. Faith trusts the Master's reward. And, what is the Master's reward for those who persevere under trial? James answers: "Blessed is a man who perseveres under trial; for once he has been approved, he will receive the crown of life which *the Lord* has promised to those who love Him" (v. 12). The word translated "approved" in the English Bible was a word used for metals and coins that had been authenticated in the fiery furnace. The end of the humble believer's trial is authentication as a child of the living God.

Real Faith and Temptation
James 1:13–16

As we learned in the opening verses of James, God puts our faith to the test. By God's sovereign design, trials make our faith stronger. However, believers who face tests may wrongly think God tempts them to do evil. James makes clear God does not lead people to sin. God tests us to bring out our best. But temptations are another matter altogether. James writes: "Let no one say when he is tempted, 'I am being tempted by God'; for God cannot be tempted by evil, and He Himself does not tempt anyone" (1:13). Just like the inevitability of tests to our faith (not "if" but "when"), the Bible warns us that we will face temptation to deny our faith—"when he is tempted."

Going all the way back to our human origins, we find ourselves blaming God for the moral mess we find ourselves in. Consider Adam when his disobedience was publicly exposed. When God inquired from him how he knew he was naked, Adam replied, "The woman whom You gave to be with me, she gave me from the tree, and I ate" (Gen. 3:12). At first Adam seems to blame Eve for his woes (and Eve blamed Satan! Gen. 3:13). Ultimately, however, Adam wasn't blaming Eve. He was blaming God! According to him, Adam's misfortune occurred because of the woman God *gave* him. And we follow our father Adam.

The truth is, we face daily temptation toward anger, dishonesty, resentment, bitterness, immorality, impurity, and countless other moral assaults against God's holy character. Unfortunately, our distorted reasoning says, "I am being tempted by God." James disputes this distorted reasoning and calls us to face up to our own self-centered needs. He insists, "Each one is tempted when he is carried away and enticed by his own lust" (Jas. 1:14). "Lust" refers to our personal but uncontrollable desire we all possess as a result of our fallen sinful nature (cp. Rom. 5:12).

In addition, our lust might have any number of objects to which it attaches itself, objects like power, pleasure, sex, money, cars, education, or material possessions in general. Accordingly, we are "carried away and enticed" by these objects (note: the objects of lust are not necessarily evil). The word translated "carried away" in the English Bible means to be "drawn" or "lured" away. Also, "enticed" originally meant "to catch by a bait."[1] Just as a worm deceives a fish to ignore the hook, so objects to which we attach our distorted desires deceive us from the dangers of our obsessions. And, according to James, the danger is real: "Then when lust has conceived, it gives birth to sin; and when sin is accomplished, it brings forth death" (1:15). The pattern is all too common.

Lust – Sin – Death

Only through genuine faith in God can believers overcome temptation. We have victory through our faith. The apostle John summed it up for us: "This is the victory that has overcome the world—our faith" (1 John 5:4).

Real Faith and Salvation
James 1:17–21

According to James, "every good thing" and "every perfect gift" comes "from above" (1:17). God is the ultimate source of all blessings whether spiritual or material. In addition, our God, who is the source of all good things, is a God who never changes. No variation exists in Him. As the author to Hebrews put it, "Jesus Christ is the same yesterday and today and forever" (Heb. 13:8).

Undoubtedly the greatest blessing bestowed on humankind is the offer of eternal salvation. James says that in exercising His will God "brought us forth by the word of truth" (1:18). The term translated "brought" means to "give rise to," "give birth to," and thus to "cause to exist" or "bring to being."[2] It is the same term used in verse 15 when James indicates that when sin is accomplished, "it brings forth death." Whereas sin kills us, God births us into existence! Moreover, James informs us how God brings us to new life in Him. We are born again "by the word of truth" (v. 18). Only through the Word of God are we saved. He uses His Word to convict us of our sin, implant faith in our hearts, lead us to Jesus, and grow us up into the likeness of His Son (1:19–20). As the apostle Paul says, "So faith comes from hearing, and hearing by the Word of Christ" (Rom. 10:17). God gives us salvation by regenerating our hearts by means of the "Word implanted" which is "able to save your souls" (1:21). The term "implanted" in the English Bible denotes to be "placed in, permanently established in, implanted."[3] God brings us permanently to new life when we are born again through His Word, and faith is the spiritual receptacle connecting us to the Word of truth.

Real Faith and the Christian Life
James 1:22–27

James understandably takes issue with cheap belief passed off as credible faith. Even the devil himself possesses cheap belief (2:19). Thus he exhorts his readers to "prove yourselves doers of the word, and not merely hearers who delude themselves" (1:22). Real faith believes something to be sure, but real faith also does something as well. Anything less is delusion.

First, real faith *hears* God. Already James has made clear that Christians must be slow to speak but swift to hear in order to receive the implantation of God's Word into their hearts (1:19). Even so, obstacles routinely stand in the way of hearing God. Hence, we must practice "putting aside all filthiness and all that remains of wickedness" (1:21) and with humble hearts listen to the Word of truth. When moral integrity is compromised, our ability to hear God takes a nosedive toward confusion and apathy. While we may still be hearing, we lose the capacity to listen, to understand. Consider the men who accompanied the apostle Paul on the Damascus Road (Acts 9:7; 22:9). They heard the voice of Jesus speaking to Saul but neither saw Jesus nor understood what He spoke. James reminds us it is possible to have good hearing but be hard of listening.

Second, in addition to hearing God with comprehension, real faith *obeys* God. That is, real faith both hears God and acts on what God says. James puts it like this: "Prove yourselves doers of the Word, and not merely hearers" (1:22). In fact, those who merely hear God but avoid doing what God says are deluded. They are not dealing with reality but only a reflection of it in a mirror. In Bible times mirrors were constructed of a flat piece of highly polished metal and used to reflect an imperfect image.[4]

We might read our Bibles every day, but if we do not obey what we read, we are no better off than the person who holds a doctor's prescription in hand but refuses to take the medicine. On the other hand, a person who gazes into the "law of liberty" and becomes "an effectual doer" will be "blessed in what he does" (v. 25). Frankly put, God blesses obedience. In addition, the phrase translated as "looks intently" in our English

Bibles makes clear that this is not a fleeting glance to which James alludes.[5] Rather, unlike a casual peek into a mirror which gives only a forgetful fuzzy reflection of reality, James implies the doer of the Word is one who bends his or her body forward indicating tension and curiosity, staring intently to understand God's perfect law.[6]

Finally, real faith *loves* others. Genuine faith never remains purely privatized. It affects both our vertical relationship with God and our horizontal relationships with others. James calls for "pure and undefiled religion" (v. 27) in contrast to "worthless" religion (v. 26). Once again James minimizes what one says and maximizes what one does. The old cliché, "Don't just talk the talk but walk the walk," profoundly promotes James' spiritual lesson. One may imagine he is "religious," but unless the tongue remains "bridled" and gracious acts are performed, deception is the final result.

In making his final thrust toward demonstrating real faith by loving others, James mentions two categories of people who solicit special concern—orphans and widows (v. 27). Orphans and widows were under special consideration in the Old Testament (Exod. 22:22; Deut. 24:17, 21; Ps. 68:5). Thus, James uses these two classes of people who often suffer unjust neglect in every culture. The term translated "visit" means much more than to show up on someone's doorstep. Oftentimes when the term is used of God, it means God showed mercy to His people by doing something merciful for them. For example, when Jesus raised the widow's son from the dead, the people's response was to glorify God because He had "visited" His people by raising a prophet among them (Luke 7:16; cp. also Luke 1:68, 78; Acts 15:14; Heb. 2:6).

Additionally, believers are to remain "unstained" by the world's moral pollution (1:27). The term "unstained" is the same term Peter uses when he speaks of the "lamb without blemish and without spot" which takes away our sins (1 Pet. 1:19, NKJV). Paul also used the term in exhorting believers to keep God's Word as it is without altering its content: "That thou keep this commandment without spot, unrebukable, until the appearing of our Lord Jesus Christ" (1 Tim. 6:14, KJV).

Thus the heart of true religion is real faith. And real faith is not cheap belief. Rather, real faith hears God, obeys God, and loves others.

For Memory and Meditation

"But one who looks intently at the perfect law, the law of liberty, and abides by it, not having become a forgetful hearer but an effectual doer, this man will be blessed in what he does." James 1:25

---

[1] W. E. Vine, Merrill F. Unger, and William White Jr., *Vine's Complete Expository Dictionary of Old and New Testament Words* (Nashville: Thomas Nelson, 1996), 58.

[2] James Swanson, *Dictionary of Biblical Languages with Semantic Domains: Greek (New Testament)* (Oak Harbor: Logos Research Systems, 1997).

[3] Johannes P. Louw and Eugene Albert Nida, *Greek-English Lexicon of the New Testament: Based on Semantic Domains* (New York: United Bible Societies, 1996), 726.

[4] Ibid., 78.

[5] Gerhard Kittel, Geoffrey W. Bromiley, and Gerhard Friedrich, eds., *Theological Dictionary of the New Testament* (Grand Rapids: Eerdmans, 1964–), 815.

[6] Ibid., footnote 13.

Christians Rendering the Royal Law

Focal Text: James 2:1–13

Many scholars rightly insist that the book of James is the oldest book in the New Testament.[1] Its chronological priority explains in part the so-called "Jewishness" in James. In some respects James is considered the New Testament version of Old Testament Proverbs.[2] Undoubtedly, James reflects a profound respect for Old Testament revelation as we shall soon see.

In the first part of James 2, James expresses his concern about partiality and favoritism gaining social traction in the Christian assembly. Overcoming such partiality and favoritism involves what he dubs the "royal law," concluding that those who fulfill it do well for their souls (2:8). After we explore the folly of favoritism (2:1–7), we'll identify the "royal law" and discover together God's instructions on loving our neighbor as ourselves.

The Folly of Favoritism
James 2:1–7

James begins this section cautioning his readers in holding their faith with some form of personal advantage (2:1). The term translated in our English Bible as "personal favoritism" denotes judgments about others based on irrelevant factors such as economic status, physical beauty, popularity, and any number of other factors, preferring instead the rich and powerful to those who are not.[3] Over and again, Scripture records God's attitude toward different people, proclaiming

19

Him to be no respecter of persons (cp. Rom. 2:11; Eph. 6:9; Col. 3:25). The apostle Peter received the same vision three different times in learning this lesson (Acts 10), a lesson he still appeared to forget at times (cp. Gal. 2:11–14).

After the initial warning about personal favoritism, James illustrates his point with a likely supposition (2:2–3). Suppose a man comes into the assembly wearing a gold ring and finely dressed followed by a poor man in dirty clothes. Who gets the "special attention" and is invited to a "good place"? James then asks, "Have you not made distinctions among yourselves, and become judges with evil motives?" (v. 4).

The term translated "assembly" (v. 2) is the term from which we get the word *synagogue*, the word used for Jewish worship assemblies. James is obviously speaking about what we refer to today as the church service. And how incredibly applicable is James' question to us! Are we not guilty at times of preferring the well-dressed middle-class over those obviously less physically or economically attractive? James concludes that when we show such preference, we've become judges with "evil motives" (v. 4). In short, our thoughts and reasons for preferring one over the other have become sorrowful and painful to God Himself.

James urges his readers to consider how much God chooses to bless the "the poor of this world" because they were so "rich in faith" (v. 5). Life's circumstances never determine the quality of one's faith in God. Thus, even people struck with poverty can be exploding with faith. And faith is the key factor in determining whether persons are "heirs of the kingdom," an inheritance promised only to those who love Him (our love for Him is demonstrated by our faith in Him).

But James' readers were in danger of dishonoring their Lord by "dishonoring the poor man" (v. 6). The term "dishonored" means to dishonor, treat shamefully, or even insult whether in word or deed.[4] When the apostles were warned about preaching Jesus and the resurrection, Luke records their response: "So they went on their way from the presence of the Council, rejoicing that they had been considered worthy to suffer shame for His name" (Acts 5:41). The term translated "suffer shame" and used to describe the apostles' treatment by the Jewish authorities is the same term James uses to describe the church's treatment of the poor man. They caused him to "suffer shame" simply because of his financial deficiencies.

James ends his treatment of this folly with a bit of irony: "Is it not the rich who oppress you and personally drag you into court? Do they not blaspheme the fair name by which you have been called?" (2:6–7). The very ones who trampled and maligned the fledging church were the ones churches escorted to the most prominent places in the worship assembly. One cannot help thinking of Jesus' words about the hypocritical Pharisees who loved to sit in the best seats at the place of worship (Matt. 23:6). The church had apparently begun playing the same game with people in their assemblies. But the folly of playing favorites in God's house called for decisive repentance. Believers must consider God's "royal law."

Identifying the Royal Law
James 2:8–9

James is clear as to what he understands the "royal law" to be. He writes: "If, however, you are fulfilling the royal law according to the Scripture, 'You shall love your neighbor as yourself,' you are doing well" (2:8). The term translated in our English Bible as "royal" denotes something "pertaining to a king—'royal, kingly.'"[5] After having put on his "royal" garments, Herod took his seat on the platform and began delivering his address to the people (Acts 12:21). Peter informed the church we were a chosen nation, a holy nation, and a "royal" priesthood (1 Pet. 2:9). James simply means the "royal" law is God's law. He's our King. He has revealed His law. And those who fulfill His law do well for themselves.

What does the "royal law" specifically say? "According to the Scripture," James says, the "royal law" is apparently summarized in a partial quote from Leviticus 19:18: "You shall love your neighbor as yourself." Could God's law be so simplistic? Consider another summation given by Jesus Himself: "'You shall love the Lord your God with all your heart, and with all your soul, and with all your mind.' This is the great and foremost commandment. The second is like it, 'You shall love your neighbor as yourself.' On these two commandments depend the whole Law and the Prophets" (Matt. 22:37–40). James seems to be closely following the interpretative precedent of His Master in summarizing the Old Testament moral code.[6] Neighbor-love was a central theme in Jesus' teaching (cp. Luke 10:30–37). Thus James' concern about how we treat people who come to our church becomes clearer when we consider the lens through which he views the issue. God's "royal law" remains as applicable to us as for Old Testament Israel!

Consequently, to breach the "royal law" was to offend its King. James cautions them that if they "show partiality" (2:9), they would be sinning against God (v. 9). Thus, they would be held accountable under the King's edict as "transgressors" (cp. also v. 11). The Greek term translated "transgressors" literally meant "to break" (cp. Rom. 2:25). And breaking the King's laws brought severe retribution.

Unity of the Royal Law
James 2:10–11

One quality of the "royal law" to bear in mind was its *unity*. James offers a stimulating statement in communicating the unity of God's law by insisting that if one law is broken, it's like all the laws are broken. He writes: "Whoever keeps the whole law and yet stumbles in one point, he has become guilty of all" (2:10). The term "whole" is a word that focuses on unity,[7] while "stumbles" indicates a fall into ruin.[8] Thus, the breach in a single commandment from the King assaults the unity of the King's authority.

James faced a unique situation. First-century Jews made distinctions between important laws and significant laws. For example, the law on Sabbath observance was particularly pressing while swearing hardly came on their radar (cp. Matt. 5:33–37; also Jas. 5:12).[9] Before we judge the Jews too harshly, let us consider how often we pick and choose between certain biblical obligations. Perhaps those biblical injunctions that are agreeable to our liking we find easy to fulfill while some that challenge our lifestyle or conscience we just as easily ignore. James' point is that we cannot choose between God's commands. God's Word is a unified whole.

But lest we think we might gain God's graces by keeping the entire law, we must forever be reminded that our Lord Jesus fulfilled the law for us (Matt. 5:17). This is not to say we are relieved of our biblical obligations to remain morally upright. It is to say, however, that our relationship to both God and His law is through faith in Jesus Christ, not through the keeping of His law (cp. Eph. 2:8–9).

The Law of Liberty
James 2:12–13

Rather than transgressing any commandment, believers should "speak and so act as those who are to be judged by the law of liberty" (2:12). The term translated "act" in our English Bibles carries the notion of expressing an action that is complete or continued. In fact, the Greek tenses of both "speak" and "act" stress a continuing form of these injunctions.[10] It's as if James says we are to be constantly speaking and always acting.

Additionally, God calls us to keep on speaking the truth and obeying His Word as one who expects to be "judged" (v. 12). We immediately note that rather than being judged by the "royal law," which James has been explaining, James summons his earlier use of "law" to encourage believers to act and live as persons who are judged by the "law of liberty" (cp. 1:25). First, even though James speaks of a "law of liberty," he by no means is speaking of some type of frivolous personal freedom to do as one pleases. After all, it is still *law* about which he speaks. But even more, James has already established the contours of Christian obedience by heavily focusing on being "doers" of the Word and not "hearers" only (1:22–25). The law of liberty sets us free not only from the world's condemnation but from being condemned by Old Testament law. Through Christ we are free indeed! (cp. John 8:36).

Recalling the poor man in the assembly who needed mercy but got only judgment and embarrassment due to the congregation's folly of favoritism, judgment must be tempered with mercy (2:13). If it is not, neither will mercy be extended to the merciless. James concludes that "mercy triumphs over judgment." Undoubtedly, he recalled the words of the Lord Jesus: "Blessed are the merciful, for they shall receive mercy" (Matt. 5:7).

For Memory and Meditation

"My brethren, do not hold your faith in our glorious Lord Jesus Christ with an attitude of personal favoritism." James 2:1

---

[1] For a critical evaluation but conservative defense of the traditional date and authorship of James, see Donald Guthrie, *New Testament Introduction*, 4th rev. ed. (Downers Grove, IL: InterVarsity Press, 1996), 722–46.

[2] Dan G. McCartney, *James*, Baker Exegetical Commentary on the New Testament (Grand Rapids: Baker Academic, 2009), 280–92.

[3] W. E. Vine, Merrill F. Unger, and William White Jr., *Vine's Complete Expository Dictionary of Old and New Testament Words* (Nashville: Thomas Nelson, 1996), 469.

[4] Ibid., 173.

[5] Johannes P. Louw and Eugene Albert Nida, *Greek-English lexicon of the New Testament: Based on Semantic Domains* (New York: United Bible

Societies, 1996), 479.

[6] James' main spiritual concern at this juncture was not vertical but horizontal. That is, he focused on Christian behavior and interpersonal relationships rather than one's salvific relationship with God. Thus, he did not mention the first and greatest commandment (love toward God) but only the second commandment (love toward neighbors) in his summation of the "royal law."

[7] Louw and Nida, *Greek-English Lexicon of the New Testament*, 612.

[8] Ibid., 773.

[9] Simon J. Kistemaker and William Hendriksen, *Exposition of James and the Epistles of John*, vol. 14, New Testament Commentary (Grand Rapids: Baker Book House, 1953–2001), 82.

[10] Douglas J. Moo, *The Letter of James*, The Pillar New Testament Commentary (Grand Rapids: Eerdmans, 2000), 116.

Faith and Works vs. Faith without Works

Focal Text: James 2:14–26

The great British Baptist, Charles Haddon Spurgeon, once answered the question, "What is faith?" this way: "Now what is faith? In one word, it is trust—the trusting of the soul in God's promise made in Christ Jesus. My faith is that which enables me to believe that God is true, to believe that he sent his Son in the flesh to suffer for my sins; to believe that, through the merit of his blood and the virtue of his holy life, I am saved. To trust in him to save me—this is faith."[1]

In short, to trust Jesus Christ is to possess biblical faith. But is this all that needs to be said concerning faith? Not according to James. In the section of Scripture before us, we are instructed not only as to what the nature of saving faith is but also how saving faith relates to our service to the Lord. The Bible calls this sanctification (cp. 1 Cor. 1:30; 1 Thess. 4:3–4).

Sanctification deals with the way the gospel affects our entire life. Since we become new creatures in Christ when we are saved (2 Cor. 5:17), our lives take on an entirely new dimension in producing fruit from this new life. At the heart of James 2:14–26 is the simple fact that genuine faith produces genuine works. If our faith is only something we talk about, James pronounces the death sentence upon it. To put it bluntly, that type of faith is dead.

Worthless Faith
James 2:14–18

First, James describes a worthless faith. He begins by asking a practical question: "What use is it, my brethren, if someone says he has faith but he has no works?" (2:14). Three key words toward understanding the nature of biblical faith are found in this passage— *say* (2:14, 16, 18); *show* (2:18); *see* (2:22, 24). All three terms imply the notion that real faith possesses recognizable evidence.

While genuine faith surely carries with it a definite verbal confession (Rom. 10:10–13), James is concerned that while some spoke well of their faith, they failed miserably in showing their faith. The term translated "use" (2:14) in the English Bible comes from a Greek root signifying "to increase" and therefore carries the notion of "advantage" or "profit."[2] Thus, James later concludes a faith that lacks works is dead (v. 17). In addition, the term "works" (v. 14) was a term routinely used to express a person's business or vocation. According to Scripture, the Christian's main vocation is to show the love of Christ and thereby bring people to Jesus.

James follows his first question with a second one which actually constitutes James' conclusion concerning a person who *says* he has faith but possesses no works to substantiate his or her claim: "Can that faith save him?" (v. 14). Many people are prone to say they possess faith. However, for James, what is a claim to have faith apart from the deeds that reveal genuine faith? As one commentator put it, "Mere profession, because of sin, does not count."[3] That kind of faith is a worthless, useless faith. John Bunyan referred to that kind of person in *Pilgrim's Progress* as "Mr. Talkative."[4] Note the example James uses to give his point some teeth. "If a brother or sister is without clothing and in need of daily food, and one of you says to them, 'Go in peace, be warmed and be filled,' and yet you do not give them what is necessary for their body, what use is that?" (vv. 15–16). The kind of demonstration James solicits is acts of kindness and mercy. Similar to his illustration at the beginning of the chapter, focus again is placed on the mistreatment of the poor and needy. The Greek word translated in the English Bible "without clothing" means "naked."[5] The obvious implication is, the need could not be missed or overlooked. It was a need that could not have "dropped through the cracks." Even more, unlike the earlier example when the needy person attending the assembly could have been an unbeliever, the naked person belongs to the church, indicated by James' reference as "brother or sister."

So, what if nothing is done to provide for the destitute brother or sister? James provides the answer in the following verse: "Even so faith, if it has no works, is dead, being by itself" (v. 17). James reasons that a person who places genuine faith in Jesus Christ is a person who possesses the desire to help others. *A said faith is a dead faith if the said faith stands alone.*

James clarifies further what he means by a dead faith with a comparison (v. 18). If an advocate of a faith *without* works would step forward, he would compare it to a faith *by* works. Undoubtedly James is thinking of something Jesus said in His sermon on the mount: "You will know them by their fruits. . . . Every tree that does not bear good fruit is cut down and thrown into the fire. So then, you will know them by their fruits" (Matt. 7:16, 19–20). Real faith inevitably produces ripe fruit.

Wicked Faith
James 2:19–20

The kind of faith James has been criticizing is the very kind of faith the evil underworld could claim. Demons are the spiritual agents acting in all forms of idolatry.[6] And demons can actually have this kind of faith: "You believe that God is one. You do well; the demons also believe, and shudder" (2:19). It is mere intellectual assent to the truth of God. James alludes to what Jews knew to be the Shema, a core doctrine of the existence of one holy God as declared in Deuteronomy 6:4: "Hear, O Israel! The LORD is our God, the LORD is one!" Christian believers confess the same doctrine of God (although Christians rightly view God as triune in nature). In other words, the belief that even demons confess is orthodox! But while it is orthodox faith, it is not active faith. Demons only believe God as factual; they do not trust God as Father. And, the truth be told, demons may well know more than any earthly religious intellectual will ever know. But even though they know all the facts about God, their belief adds up to nothing but raw fear. The word translated in the English Bible as "shudder" (2:19) means "to bristle" and carries the notion of having one's hair stand on end[7] (cp. Matt. 8:29).

Consequently, while the demons' theology (belief about God) is impeccable, their possession of real faith remains negligible. What may assist us in seeing James' point is to consider that the devil himself could join the average church. He believes in Jesus; he knows the Scriptures; he believes in the resurrection from the dead, the virgin birth, prophecy, and even baptism. Demons are not atheists or agnostics. Rather they firmly believe in the deity of Jesus Christ! Even so, James reminds us, the kind of faith demons have is no worse than the kind of faith some of his readers possessed who claimed faith but lacked works. Once again, only a fool would fail to grasp that "faith without works is useless" (2:20).

Worthy Faith
James 2:21–26

Thus far we've noted both a *worthless* faith (2:14–18) and a *wicked* faith (2:19–20). A person who says on the one hand he or she possesses faith but demonstrates no visible evidence to substantiate the claim is more than likely holding a worthless belief. In fact, according to James, demons possess a faith that remains worthless because it only offers mental assent to the truth. Consequently, we can dub this kind of faith *wicked* because the satanic underworld regularly exercises this kind of subbiblical belief. And the truth is, countless people hold the same belief as the demons. While they know the truth, they refuse to be changed by the truth.

James now turns our attention to *worthy* faith. What is a worthy faith? Are there valid criteria we can examine to discern whether we possess worthy faith rather than the two inferior faiths he's already described? James gives us a resounding "Yes!" and begins by declaring that a worthy faith is a *witnessing* faith. Drawing from an Old Testament hero of faith, James writes, "Was not Abraham our father justified by works when he offered up Isaac his son on the altar? You see that faith was working with his works, and as a result of the works, faith was perfected" (2:21–22). James' readers would have instantly identified with Abraham as an example of faith, for the patriarch was considered in the New Testament era as the father of all who believe (cp. Rom. 4:16; Gal. 3:6–7, 9). By faith Abraham had settled his sin account in full before the Almighty (Rom. 4:3; Gal. 3:6). God justified him, and he received a righteousness based on faith not law (cp. Rom. 4:13).

Some have confused what James recorded in 2:21 concerning being "justified by works" with what the apostle Paul declared in Romans 3:20; namely, "Because by the works of the Law no flesh will be justified in His sight" (cp. Rom. 3:28; 4:2; Gal. 2:16). On the surface this sounds like a direct contradiction. In fact, Martin Luther, a key player during the Protestant Reformation of the sixteenth century, initially rejected the book of James, calling it an "epistle of straw."[8] The chief criteria for Luther was he believed James 2:21 directly contradicted the apostle Paul's clear teaching that justification before God comes through faith alone and without the works of the law (cp. Rom. 3:28).

The key to understanding what both James and Paul mean centers in some respects on the two different ways each use the term *justify*. The apostle Paul specifically uses the term in a sense concerning the way a person actually comes into right relationship with God. However, James (who wrote before Paul) uses the term *justify* in an entirely different sense. James is not concerned about how an unsaved sinner rightly relates himself or herself to God. Rather James uses the term *justify* in a sense of *vindicating* one's faith before men.

New Testament scholar Douglas Moo is spot on: "So 'justify' in Paul refers to how a person gets into relationship with God, while in James it connotes what that relationship must ultimately look like to receive God's final approval."[9] We could say it like this: *Paul concerns himself with the root of salvation while James concerns himself with the fruit of salvation.* Viewed in this sense, no contradiction whatsoever remains. And Abraham's "works" vindicated his possession of worthy faith. In short, his testimony of "works" served as credible evidence his witness to a saving faith in Jesus Christ remained authentic.

Not only does James indicate worthy faith is a *witnessing* faith, but a worthy faith is also a *winning* faith (2:23). Faith alone had established Abraham as a child of God, but through his works his faith was fulfilled making him a "friend of God" (cp. 2 Chron. 20:7; Isa. 41:8). Being God's friend is one of the most precious biblical descriptors for believers. Scripture likens the conversation Moses could have with the God of Israel as the way one friend speaks to another (Exod. 33:11). Jesus is described as friend to publicans and sinners (Luke 7:34). Even more, He calls His followers His friends for whom He lays down His life (John 15:13–15). A worthy faith is a winning faith because it is fulfilled (i.e. vindicated) through works.

Consequently, James now indicates clearly that a

worthy faith will ever remain a *working* faith: "You see that a man is justified by works and not by faith alone" (2:24). Keep in mind James' use of the term "justified" as described above. Again, a person is rightly related to God on the basis of faith alone, but his or her faith is only vindicated before the watching world through the works visibly performed before them.

Another key player in the Reformation was John Calvin. Along with other Reformers, Calvin famously indicated that "justification is by faith alone, but not by a faith that is alone"[10] What does this mean? James means a saving faith—a *worthy* faith—will always be a working faith. Fruit will inevitably be a by-product when saving faith is present. While some people could produce good deeds in the sight of men, thus masquerading as a genuine believer when no saving faith is present, no person can possess saving faith without also producing faith-vindicating works. The famous evangelist of the nineteenth century, D. L. Moody, reportedly said, "Every Bible should be bound in shoe-leather."[11]

Adding to Abraham, James hurls yet another example of worthy faith. But this time the example is not as readily identifiable as was Abraham. Drawing from Joshua's beginning conquest of the promised land (Josh. 2:4, 6, 15), James cites Rahab as a second example of worthy faith (2:25; cp. also Heb. 11:31). The central point he makes seals the specific use of being "justified." Rahab's faith in the God of Moses vindicated itself through her "works" of assisting Joshua's scouts to escape both capture and doom. Hence, Rahab's faith was real faith; it was biblical faith; it was saving faith.

For as James concludes, a faith without the accompanying works to vindicate it before the world is dead (2:26).

For Mediation and Memory

"For just as the body without *the* spirit is dead, so also faith without works is dead." James 2:26

---

[1] C. H. Spurgeon, *The Metropolitan Tabernacle Pulpit Sermons*, vol. LXI (London: Passmore & Alabaster, 1915), 176.

[2] W. E. Vine, Merrill F. Unger, and William White Jr., *Vine's Complete Expository Dictionary of Old and New Testament Words* (Nashville: Thomas Nelson, 1996), 15.

[3] Kurt A. Richardson, *James*, vol. 36, The New American Commentary (Nashville: B&H, 1997), 128.

[4] Geo Offor, ed., Introduction by the Editor, *The Pilgrim's Progress*, vol. 3 (Bellingham, WA: Logos Bible Software, 2006), 69.

[5] Douglas J. Moo, *The Letter of James*, The Pillar New Testament Commentary (Grand Rapids: Eerdmans, 2000) 124.

[6] Vine, Unger, and White Jr., *Vine's Complete Expository Dictionary of Old and New Testament Words*, 158.

[7] Spiros Zodhiates, *The Complete Word Study Dictionary: New Testament* (Chattanooga, TN: AMG Publishers, 2000).

[8] Philip Schaff and David Schley Schaff, *History of the Christian Church* (New York: Charles Scribner's Sons, 1910). Fortunately Luther later recanted his views.

[9] Douglas J. Moo, *The Letter of James*, The Pillar New Testament Commentary (Grand Rapids: Eerdmans, 2000) 135.

[10] R. C. Sproul, *Faith Alone: The Evangelical Doctrine of Justification*, electronic ed. (Grand Rapids: Baker Books, 2000) 155.

[11] As quoted in Warren W. Wiersbe, *The Bible Exposition Commentary* (Wheaton, IL: Victor Books, 1996), Col. 1:10.

Do Our Words Injure or Inspire?

Focal Text: James 3:1–12

James has been called the wisdom book of the New Testament similar to Proverbs in the Old Testament (see lesson 1). A recurring theme in Proverbs focuses on the use of one's words. "My son, give attention to my words," says the inspired sage (Prov. 4:20). Cautioning his hearers to avoid needless babble, he writes: "When there are many words, transgression is unavoidable, but he who restrains his lips is wise" (10:19). Finally, he warns, "Do not speak in the hearing of a fool, for he will despise the wisdom of your words" (23:9). These three texts serve as a mere sampling of the dozens of texts in Proverbs exhorting us to use our words wisely and to speak our words cautiously and encouragingly. Hence, we should not be surprised to find in James recurring themes pertaining to the use of the human language whether good or bad (cp. 1:19; 2:12; 3:10–13; 4:11).

James begins on a positive note, suggesting the honorable contributions of those who teach. Even so, he adds a specific warning to discourage insincere candidates for the teaching role since explaining the Word of God inaccurately can be detrimental to the health of the New Testament church.

Biblical Teacher: Positive Role but Precautionary Measures
James 3:1

James writes: "Let not many *of you* become teachers, my brethren, knowing that as such we will incur a stricter judgment" (3:1). The "stricter judgment" James indicates is the expected criteria every would-be teacher faces in God's future judgment. Hence, in a roundabout way James declares the significance the teacher possesses in God's church. The term translated "stricter" in the English Bible means something great and large, particularly of physical magnitude.[1] We get our term *mega* from this Greek word as in "mega-church."[2] In short, James reminds those who desire to teach God's Word to others that they must face a "mega" judgment at the last day.

Teaching constituted a primary factor from the beginning of the New Testament church. Jesus preached His most famous sermon on the Mount of Olives—the Sermon on the Mount. Matthew describes it like this: "He opened His mouth and taught them" (Matt. 5:2, NKJV). What caught the scribes' and Pharisees' attention was Jesus *teaching* with an authority they had never experienced (Matt. 7:29; 13:54). Mark reminds us that Jesus went all over Galilee *teaching* the people (Mark 6:6). When the apostles were threatened with their lives for speaking of Jesus and the resurrection, it was reported to the religious leaders that those whom they put in prison are "standing in the temple and *teaching* the people!" (Acts 5:25). In fact, teaching was already established as the core of apostolic ministry: "They were continually devoting themselves to the apostles' teaching and to fellowship, to the breaking of bread and to prayer" (Acts 2:42).

In some of the later books of the New Testament, when the church was more organized, we find the apostle Paul instructing the church to make sure teaching was a vital part of the ministry. To Titus he insisted that he hold fast "the faithful word which is in accordance with the teaching" in order to "exhort in sound doctrine" as well as to "refute" those uninstructed in the faith (Titus 1:9). Paul instructed Timothy to entrust the apostolic faith to "faithful men who will be able to teach others also" (2 Tim. 2:2). Finally, in securing pastors for leading local churches, Paul included a catalog of criteria concerning the suitable candidate the church should pursue (1 Tim. 3:1–7). The spiritual qualifications for local church pastors include not only godly character (2:2–3) but also stable leadership in the home (2:4–5). In addition, the local church pastor must possess a good reputation even from those outside the church (3:7). A pastoral candidate also must be settled in the faith and not an inexperienced novice (3:7).

For our purposes, however, Paul insists the credentialed local church pastor must "able to teach" (1 Tim. 3:2). To demonstrate how the ability to teach served as a nonnegotiable qualification for the New Testament pastor, one need only compare the qualifications for pastors in 1 Timothy 3:1–7 with the qualifications for deacons in 1 Timothy 3:8–13. The similarities are striking for the pastor on one hand and the deacons on the other. Nonetheless one criterion present for the pastor is absent for qualified deacons—"able to teach" (3:2). Indicated here is the unqualified significance teaching played in the formation of the New Testament church. *Pastors must be teachers.*

Little wonder James reminds his readers to avoid the temptation to teach unless he or she is willing to face the "mega" responsibility of instructing souls in the kingdom of God. While surely James' injunction solicits reluctance on the part of those desiring to teach, his purpose is not to discourage but to raise awareness that the role of teaching is not to be taken lightly. No one is infallible; nor does God expect us to be. But since words are the teacher's primary tool, teachers face greater responsibility for their kingdom service because of the powerful position teaching provides in influencing others' lives.

Power of Words to Direct One's Life
James 3:3–5a

James himself possessed an incredible gift for teaching. Often we can discern in his exhortations everyday illustrations from the daily grind of life. In this brief section James employs three colorful images to depict the undeniable control words have over people. The first image is a horse's bit. He writes, "Now if we put the bits into the horses' mouths so that they will obey us, we direct their entire body as well" (3:3). Primitive bridles were simply a "loop on the halter cord passed round the lower jaw of the horse. Hence in Ps. 32:9 the meaning is bridle and halter."[3] Bridles control the entire direction of the animal. So do our tongues, James reminds us. By words, life is steered for both good and bad. Hence we must be careful which words we use. Later James denies that both sweet water and bitter water come from the same well (3:10–12).

The second image James uses to illustrate what a controlling factor words have is a ship's rudder (3:4). Consider the size of the massive merchant ships of the ancient world; yet the tiny rudder not only shifts the direction of the ship any way the captain commands, but it may stabilize the ship during violent storms which routinely come. The rudder possesses the potential and power to control and influence something many times its size. So the tongue—our words—comparatively influence our lives though it is a small portion of our body. Controlling the rudder controls the ship. The application is obvious: controlling our words controls the direction not only of our lives but also of the lives of others.

The final image James uses is a "small part" indicating the melody of music.[4] The underlying notion is composing a song. The "small part" must be in harmony with other instruments else no control can be performed on the song itself. In short, it becomes a mangled mess of meaningless chords on instruments all playing at the same time. Misusing words makes our lives into an incoherent musical no one enjoys. Only disharmony and discord follow.

Power of Words to Destroy One's Life
James 3:5b–8

Words not only have power to direct life, but they also have the potential to destroy a person's life. James likens words to the strike of a match, which sets off a forest fire burning uncontrollably. He warns: "See how great a forest is set aflame by such a small fire!" (3:5). A tiny fire begins a gigantic flame. It took only a single spark to ignite the hydrogen on the outer skin of the giant *Hindenburg* airship, which had ninety-five passengers on board, as it floated slowly to the ground while engulfed in flames. Thirty-six people died in the 1937 disaster. Just as a spark destroys, so do a person's words if not controlled.

Therefore, the tongue is the "very world of iniquity" (v. 6). The word translated "world" carries the notion of a great sum of something, implying an almost incredible totality; that is, "a world of, a tremendous amount of."[5] James seems to be saying our tongues potentially are the symbol of evil or a sign of what is truly evil. We simply cannot underestimate its wretched capabilities. No other part of our body has the same capacity for destruction as our tongues.

Someone reportedly once said to John Wesley: "I pride myself in speaking my mind. That is my talent."

The Methodist revivalist replied, "Well, the Lord wouldn't mind if you buried that talent."

No amount of rationalizing can reduce James' utter disgust for the destructive powers of speech. But he was only following the disgust he knew from the Wisdom literature of the Old Testament. For example, in Proverbs 6:16, Solomon records, "There are six things which the LORD hates, yes, seven which are an abomination to Him." Of the seven things God hates and judges abominable, three have to do with speech: "a lying tongue" (6:17), "a false witness" (6:19), and "spread[ing] strife" (6:19). James forged his views on the tongue from the pages of God's Word in the Old Testament.

Thus, for James, the tongue potentially "defiles the entire body" (3:6). The term translated in the English Bible as "defiles" comes from a Greek term from which we get our word *spill*. When coffee spills on our newly laundered shirt, it leaves a spot, the literal meaning of "defiles."[6] Note what Jude writes concerning garments which are "polluted by the flesh" (Jude 23).[7] The tongue potentially pollutes our lives driving us into all sorts of confusion.

In addition to pollution, James says our tongue "is set on fire by hell" (3:6). The term translated "hell" ultimately comes from two Hebrew words that meant "Valley of Hinnom."[8] Just outside the city of Jerusalem, a valley lay which earned an evil reputation centuries earlier. Child sacrifices were carried out in the valley in honor of pagan deities (cp. Jer. 32:35). Moreover, not only garbage was burned there in the first century, but the corpses of dead animals and even some humans were disposed of in the valley. Jesus used "hell" in referencing the ultimate judgment and destiny of unrepentant sinners. In fact, Christ is the only one to use the same Greek word as James uses here. For James the tongue's destructive forces are motivated and encouraged by none other than hell itself.

Consequently, it becomes crystal clear why no person gains control over the tongue. Contrary to other creatures men have been able to tame (3:7), the tongue remains nothing less than a "restless evil" which is "full of deadly poison," a creation "no one can tame" (v. 8). The term "restless" signifies the impossibility of keeping something in check. The term translated "poison" is the same term Paul uses in Romans 3:3 referring to the poisonous venom of snakes. Thus, the uncontrolled tongue flows through one's life like the poisonous venom of a snakebite flows through one's bloodstream, spreading destruction with every beat of the heart.

Power of Words to Disclose One's Life
James 3:9–12

Words possess the power not only to direct through sound teaching, but also to destroy through sinful misuse. James ends his exhortation on the powerful potential our little member has by suggesting the tongue's ability to disclose what our lives actually are but ought not to be. He writes: "With it we bless our Lord and Father, and with it we curse men . . . ; from the same mouth come both blessing and cursing. My brethren, these things ought not to be this way" (3:9–10). First, James observes the inconsistencies we too frequently embrace in the use of our tongue. On the one hand we rightly bless God with the words we speak. God calls our speech the "sacrifice of praise" which is the "fruit of [our] lips" (Heb. 13:15). But the discrepancy begins when we curse men who are "made in the likeness of God" (3:9). James' use of the term translated "likeness" remains the only instance of its use in the New Testament.[9] Obviously he reflects back to the creation narrative when God made Adam and Eve in His own image and likeness (Gen. 1:26). Though sinned marred God's image in us, sin did not make us less than human. We still bear God's image. Indeed God's image in man became the substantial defense for human life beginning at conception.

What does it mean to be made in God's likeness? In short, it means we have intellectual, moral, and psychological powers no other creature on the planet possesses. We are decidedly unique among God's created order. But our uniqueness brings added responsibilities, one responsibility of which is to treat others with a

44

visible measure of respect and dignity. Why? Because, like us, they too are made in God's likeness.

Therefore, to curse another human being is to assault God's character through the back door, so to speak. James is clear: "These things ought not to be this way" (3:10). He illustrates the absurdity of cursing and blessing coming from the same source by alluding to a fountain (v. 11) and a fig tree (v. 12). "How could both sweet water and bitter water flow from the same brook?" he asks. Similarly, "How do fig trees produce anything but figs?" Neither should we expect such impossible duplicities to exist among Christian brothers and sisters, all of whom are made in God's likeness.

For Memory and Mediation

"Let not many of you become teachers, my brethren, knowing that as such we will incur a stricter judgment." James 3:1

[1] Spiros Zodhiates, *The Complete Word Study Dictionary: New Testament* (Chattanooga, TN: AMG Publishers, 2000).

[2] Since the early 1980s, we've routinely identified megachurches as churches that have two thousand or more in attendance.

[3] *Hastings Dictionary of the Bible*, as quoted in W. E. Vine, Merrill F. Unger, and William White Jr., *Vine's Complete Expository Dictionary of Old and New Testament Words* (Nashville: Thomas Nelson, 1996), 79.

[4] Johnny Hunt, *The Book of James: First and Second Edition: an Archive of Exegetical Sermon Notes* (Woodstock: 3H Publishers, 2011), 74.

[5] Johannes P. Louw and Eugene Albert Nida, *Greek-English Lexicon of the New Testament: Based on Semantic Domains* (New York: United Bible Societies, 1996), 599.

[6] Zodhiates, *The Complete Word Study Dictionary: New Testament*.

[7] The KJV captures the Greek word perfectly when it translates the word for "polluted" as "spotted."

[8] Douglas J. Moo, *The Letter of James*, The Pillar New Testament Commentary (Grand Rapids: Eerdmans, 2000), 159–60.

[9] Zodhiates, *The Complete Word Study Dictionary: New Testament*.

Get Wisdom

Focal Text: James 3:13–18

The great preacher of last century, A. W. Tozer, said: "We need to learn and to declare again the mystery of wisdom from above. Truth consists not merely in correct doctrine but in correct doctrine to which is added the inward enlightenment of the Holy Spirit."[1] Tozer was on to something. Skill, intellectual capacity, and the mere collection of raw data are insufficient to successfully navigate through life's treacherous waters. Instead we must obtain a certain measure of heavenly wisdom to safely arrive on shore.

If believers are to excel in their walk with Christ, they must learn not only how to get wisdom but also how to get the right kind of wisdom. As the text unfolds, we will discover wisdom comes in at least two varieties—wisdom from above and wisdom from below. How do we know we have the right wisdom? What criteria exist to protect us from the wrong kind of wisdom?

Developing a Heart to Nurture Wisdom
James 3:13–14

James has already exhorted believers to exercise godly wisdom; and for those who lack it, they need only "ask" and God will graciously grant their request (1:5). The only condition is asking in faith (1:6). In addition, James' focus on wisdom remains another indication he's following Old Testament Wisdom literature in composing his letter. "Acquire wisdom! Acquire understanding! Do not forget nor turn away from the words of my mouth. . . . The beginning of wisdom is: Acquire wisdom; and with all your acquiring, get understanding" (Prov. 4:5, 7). For Solomon, "Fools despise wisdom and instruction" (Prov. 1:7). According to Paul, the Lord Jesus has become to us "wisdom from God" (1 Cor. 1:30).

Therefore, James again calls on the church to seek wisdom from God. He begins by asking a question: "Who among you is wise and understanding?" (3:13). In Greek culture the term translated "wise" was used to describe learned men like Plato and Aristotle. But in the New Testament the term took on a different meaning.[2] First, wisdom according to Scripture is rooted in God's character rather than in man's character or accomplishments. Thus, neither brilliance nor training necessarily contributes to wisdom's presence or absence. Furthermore, to possess wisdom is also to possess understanding. Acquiring understanding presumes one has already acquired wisdom. And understanding carries a practical dimension along with it. In other words, to be wise describes a person with moral insight and sharpened skill in deciding practical matters relating to life. A person gains this wisdom as a direct result of having a relationship with God.

Now that James has asked who might be the wise and understanding person among them, he commences to offer an answer: "Let him show by his good behavior his deeds in the gentleness of wisdom" (v. 13). Note two particular points James expresses. First, our *actions* demonstrate whether wisdom is present. The wise person is to "show" wisdom exists by "good behavior" and "deeds." The term translated "show" carries the notion of an exhibition like when the devil took our Lord upon the mountain and showed Him all the world's kingdoms (Matt. 4:8).[3] Thus the wise person exhibits wisdom through good behavior. Again biblical wisdom is connected to practical action. Our behavior indicates whether wisdom exists. While some might be intellectually brilliant, they might also qualify, so far as Scripture is concerned to be foolish and destructive.

Second, our *attitudes* also demonstrate wisdom. James says acts are performed in the "gentleness of wisdom" (3:13). The term "gentleness" denotes the attitude of our behavior as being gentle, meek, and even mild.[4] Thus, not only are the acts themselves considered good, but the inner frame of mind and heart while performing the act tells a story all its own. Unlike today when this attitude is frequently judged to be weak and spineless, humility reflects the inner working of the Holy Spirit.

By focusing on our attitudes, James indicates the type of inner environment necessary to nurture both the presence and the growth of wisdom displayed in our lives. He states even stronger the condition in which our hearts must be in order for wisdom to function properly: "But if you have bitter jealousy and selfish ambition in your heart, do not be arrogant and so lie against the truth" (v. 14). If wisdom is going to operate in the believer's life, then he or she must begin with a cleansed vessel.

The term translated "bitter" James has already used to describe the bitter spring water "brackish to the taste" (see 3:12; cp. also Rev. 8:11; 10:9).[5] The word here probably refers to violent or even uncontrollable sentiments settled in a person's heart (cp. Luke 22:62). Bitterness becomes a deadly poison to healthy relationships. The apostle Paul typified sin's universal expression as being filled with bitterness (Rom. 3:14) and exhorted the Ephesians to "let all bitterness . . . be put away from you" (Eph. 4:31). Thus, wisdom cannot thrive where bitterness grows.

But it's not just bitterness James has in his sights, but bitter "jealousy." Desiring the good of one's brother or sister is replaced by desiring destruction. So envious has this person become toward the success of a fellow Christian that an uncontrollable, violent envy dominates which seeks the downfall of one of God's children. A more twisted passion can hardly be imagined. Wisdom has no future in a heart like this. Truth be told, envy was undoubtedly the sin involved in the usurpation of the knowledge of good and evil that belonged to God when Eve gave in to the serpent's temptation (Gen. 3:1–7) just as envy of the rich man's wealth stood as the root of partiality which James earlier addressed (2:1–4).[6] Envy drains away any chance that wisdom will sprout.

In addition, where "selfish ambition" grows, godly wisdom inevitably remains choked. "Selfish ambition" comes from a single Greek word denoting a desire to put oneself forward in a partisan or fractious spirit.[7] It was used before the New Testament era to describe self-interested politicians who spoke and acted in ways that benefited only themselves. If persons are more interested in preserving self than in adoring God, wisdom will hardly find the suitable soil necessary to grow and thrive.

The term translated "arrogant" is a strengthened and intensified form of a verb that means to boast.[8] A person who possesses wisdom knows he or she never could possess it apart from God's grace active in his or her life. James' insight remains a remarkable challenge to those who presume to be wise in doing God's work but inwardly are driven by pride, arrogance, and selfish ambition so that our lives are aimed at destroying those we envy.[9]

Discerning Different Kinds of Wisdom
James 3:15–18

Now that James has developed the kind of mind and heart conducive to implementing wisdom from God, he drives his point deeper still by showing the differences between two kinds of wisdom. Some wisdom comes from above, but there is also wisdom he suggests has origins foreign to heaven.

Wisdom from Below (3:15–16)

James describes the kind of wisdom manufactured on earth rather than descending from heaven: "This wisdom is not that which comes down from above, but is earthly, natural, demonic" (3:15). Three descriptors are used to define humanly inspired wisdom. First, James says this wisdom is "earthly." The term was used to denote things that existed on earth or belonging to earth in contrast to what is not on earth.[10] For example, Paul said that if our "earthly" body ceased to exist ("were dissolved"), then we would be furnished a "building from God, a house not made with hands, eternal in the heavens" (2 Cor. 5:1). Remember, James has already assured us God is willing to send His wisdom from heaven to those who ask in faith (1:5–8).

Thus God's wisdom not only is possible to obtain, but it is confidently promised to the faithful disciple of the Lord Jesus. How tragic it is when believers settle for "earthly" wisdom when heaven's is available. According to Jesus, that which is born of flesh is flesh (John 3:6). So we have every reason to believe wisdom born of the flesh bears all the earmarks of sinful tendencies latent within our flesh. Too frequently Christians attempt to rely on "earthly" wisdom by focusing on developing skill sets, acquiring knowledge, heeding advice from pop psychologists, or following the latest and greatest trends originating from culture. Yet one common thread stitches every one of these wisdom sources together—"earthly." As James says, "This wisdom is not that which comes down from above" (3:15).

Second, James describes the wisdom from below as "natural." The term translated "natural" in our English Bibles pertains to the life of the natural world and whatever belongs to it in contrast to the realm of the spirit.[11] James acknowledges that even sinful creatures are capable of producing wisdom, but the wisdom produced only accounts for the natural world and not the spiritual world. Wisdom from above is godly wisdom, *spiritual* wisdom.

Third, James describes wisdom from below not only as "earthly" and "natural" but, even more troubling, as "demonic." In other words, James indicts wisdom from this world as proceeding from demons themselves.[12] What possible reason could more inspire believers to reject wisdom from this world by getting on their knees and asking wisdom from God than the realization that the wisdom from below comes from hell? Chapter 3 began with James' warning about taking the teaching role seriously (v. 1). It led to a discussion of the evils of an uncontrolled tongue. Now James informs us of the ultimate reason. Hell itself inspires ungodly wisdom even foolish Christians may follow.[13]

How may we discern the presence of demonic wisdom? James explains that the presence of "jealousy and selfish ambition" remains key to understanding the presence of demonic wisdom (v. 16). False wisdom always supports and encourages self-assertion and independence. Mutual concern can hardly thrive in a context where self-interest reigns; where believers "do their own thing," so to speak, instead of building a godly community of loving support.[14] Demonic wisdom supports jealous, selfish pursuits ending in what James calls "disorder and every evil thing" (v. 16).

Wisdom from Above (3:17–18)

After defining wisdom from below, James now offers a catalog of virtues describing the wisdom God graciously gives to those who ask in faith (cp. 1:5–6). By listing eight descriptors, James explains what heaven's wisdom looks like (3:17).

Pure—James says wisdom from God is "first, pure." Whether he means to suggest purity is the prominent virtue when considering God's wisdom or that purity is merely the first of many virtues when considering wisdom from above is hard to tell. Baptist Greek scholar A. T. Robertson suggested that by speaking of

God's wisdom being "pure," James meant purity to be first in both rank and time.[15] The word denotes being pure from any fault. Hence, God's wisdom cannot be half good and half bad. Rather wisdom from above is singularly good and unmixed with any taint of evil whatsoever.

Peaceable—This term means to be at peace and to live in peace.[16] Peace will play an important part in applying God's wisdom when James speaks about the "fights" among the church members in the next portion of Scripture (4:1, NKJV). God's wisdom settles disputes once and for all.

Gentle—God's wisdom is both courteous and tolerant, but that does not mean His wisdom is either weak or lily-livered. James earlier exhorted the church to be quick in hearing while slow in verbal retaliation, concluding that "the anger of man does not achieve the righteousness of God" (1:20). Paul also encouraged believers to speak the truth while doing so in love (Eph. 4:15). James followed Old Testament wisdom which reasoned, "A gentle answer turns away wrath, but a harsh word stirs up anger" (Prov. 15:1).

Reasonable—We may be tempted to equate James' term with a high esteem for strict logic to which he may have alluded. James, however, was not thinking of formal logic. The term he uses denotes "easily obeying" or being "compliant."[17] Thus, being reasonable is more like what we mean by being agreeable in the contrasting sense of being ornery or disagreeable. It's an old cliché but perhaps captures it well: *agreeing to disagree agreeably*.

Full of mercy and good fruits—God's wisdom produces ample mercy and positive fruits. Leniency and grace characterize wisdom from above.

Unwavering—Once again, given our normal usage of the English rendering, we may be tempted to draw the lines around James' meaning much too narrowly. While we may think to be unwavering simply means to "stick to one's guns," James means more. He's not so much referencing someone who never wavers on a decision as he is not being judgmental, divisive, or impartial.[18] In a real sense James says wisdom from above would never have treated a poor man like they were treating a poor man (2:1–7). Thus, wisdom from below operated in their fellowship, not wisdom from above.

Without hypocrisy—Contrary to uncharitable partiality, wisdom from above thrives on authentic Christian community as was exhorted earlier in obeying the royal law of loving one's neighbor as oneself (2:8). No one spoke stronger words than our Lord Jesus pertaining to His disgust for visible hypocrisy (cp. Matt. 23:1–36). Wisdom from above remains void of insincerity.

For Memory and Mediation

"But the wisdom from above is first pure, then peaceable, gentle, reasonable, full of mercy and good fruits, unwavering, without hypocrisy." James 3:17

---

[1] A. W. Tozer and Gerald B. Smith, *Men Who Met God* (Camp Hill, PA: Wing-Spread, 1986), 124.

[2] Spiros Zodhiates, *The Complete Word Study Dictionary: New Testament* (Chattanooga, TN: AMG Publishers, 2000).

[3] W. E. Vine, Merrill F. Unger, and William White Jr., *Vine's Complete Expository Dictionary of Old and New Testament Words* (Nashville: Thomas Nelson, 1996), 569.

[4] Johannes P. Louw and Eugene Albert Nida, *Greek-English Lexicon of*

the New Testament: Based on Semantic Domains (New York: United Bible Societies, 1996), 748.

[5] Gerhard Kittel, Geoffrey W. Bromiley, and Gerhard Friedrich, eds., Theological Dictionary of the New Testament (Grand Rapids: Eerdmans, 1964–), 124.

[6] Kurt A. Richardson, James, vol. 36, The New American Commentary (Nashville: B&H, 1997), 164.

[7] James Strong, Enhanced Strong's Lexicon (Bellingham, WA: Logos Bible Software, 2001).

[8] John F. MacArthur Jr., James, MacArthur New Testament Commentary (Chicago: Moody Press, 1998), 171.

[9] R. Kent Hughes, James: Faith That Works, Preaching the Word (Wheaton, IL: Crossway Books, 1991), 152.

[10] Kittel, Bromiley, and Friedrich, eds., Theological Dictionary of the New Testament, 680.

[11] William Arndt, Frederick W. Danker, and Walter Bauer, A Greek-English Lexicon of the New Testament and Other Early Christian Literature (Chicago: University of Chicago Press, 2000), 1,100.

[12] Timothy Friberg, Barbara Friberg, and Neva F. Miller, Analytical Lexicon of the Greek New Testament, Baker's Greek New Testament Library (Grand Rapids: Baker Books, 2000), 103.

[13] Peter H. Davids, The Epistle of James: a Commentary on the Greek Text, New International Greek Testament Commentary (Grand Rapids: Eerdmans, 1982), 153.

[14] Thomas D. Lea, Hebrews, James, vol. 10, Holman New Testament Commentary (Nashville: B&H, 1999), 307.

[15] A. T. Robertson, Word Pictures in the New Testament (Nashville: Broadman, 1933).

[16] Ceslas Spicq and James D. Ernest, Theological Lexicon of the New Testament (Peabody, MA: Hendrickson Publishers, 1994), 424.

[17] Joseph Henry Thayer, A Greek-English Lexicon of the New Testament: Being Grimm's Wilke's Clavis Novi Testamenti (New York: Harper & Brothers., 1889), 261.

[18] Arndt, Danker, and Bauer, A Greek-English Lexicon of the New Testament and Other Early Christian Literature, 19.

Corrupt Desires

Focal Text: James 4:1–6

Charles Haddon Spurgeon once indicated his longing for the moment "when all evil affections, corrupt desires, and rebellious, doubting thoughts shall be overcome, and completely crushed beneath the Prince's feet, and my whole soul be made pure and holy. But so long as I am encaged within this house of clay, I know they will lurk about, and I must have hard fighting though the victory by grace is sure. Praying is the best fighting; nothing else will keep them down."[1] Spurgeon remained much aware of the conflicts *without* being rooted deep *within* the soul. He also knew the Christian's secret—prayer.

James 4:1–5 addresses the source of conflict we so often ignore—misguided personal preferences. Even more James offers believers a sure remedy for dealing with corrupted desires. In short, we must learn how to pray without praying amiss.

Desires that Control Us
James 4:1

This chapter begins with James asking two rhetorical questions: "What is the source of quarrels and conflicts among you? Is not the source your pleasures that wage war in your members?" He uses two different words pertaining to war in order to paint a broad swath concerning the battle he's describing. The former word ("quarrels") denotes an overall campaign while the latter word ("conflicts") refers more to a local engagement. More importantly is the tragic arena where the war takes place—"among you." The church is the battleground James addresses.

The "quarrels and conflicts" among God's people speak of continuous wrangling spawned by resentment and bitterness within people's hearts. Thus, the source of visible trouble in the church is invisible trouble in the heart. James makes this clear in his second rhetorical question. Doesn't the outward conflict come from your desires for "pleasures that wage war in your members"? James sends a powerful message to the church concerning the destructiveness of relationships where violent attitudes have broken out unchecked.[2] Whereas now a lack of compassion demonstrated the church's partisan favoritism (2:1–7), their visible hostility in warring and fighting among one another reveals the sad state of their hearts.

The Christian's struggle with his or her own questionable desires plays a prominent role in the New Testament. The apostle Paul speaks of our struggle in terms of flesh against spirit and spirit against flesh (Gal. 5:17). He furthered noted that when we lived "in the flesh" our "sinful passions . . . were at work in the members of our body to bear fruit for death" (Rom. 7:5). Thus, we are called to put to death our flesh so that Christ may live through us. Paul says it like this: "For if you are living according to the flesh, you must die; but if by the Spirit you are putting to death the deeds of the body, you will live" (Rom. 8:13). Indeed the assurance we get from God is that if we walk in the Spirit we won't fulfill the lusts of our flesh (Gal. 5:16).

The fundamental struggle James addresses begins

within a person's heart. External struggles displayed in the church are indicative of internal struggles going on in our hearts. Aside from the partisan favoritism practiced in the church (2:1–7), the people James addressed also struggled with public notoriety (indicative in the overt desire to become "teachers," 3:1), envy and selfish ambition (3:14, 16), and fruitless hypocrisy (3:9–10). Thus, virtually all of the problems James has countered heretofore may be summarized as problems of the heart. Corrupted desires had taken control.

Jesus often warned about desires of this world. In the parable of the sower (Luke 8:4–15), Jesus said the seed that fell among thorns brought no fruit because they were "choked with worries and riches and pleasures of this life" (v. 14). Paul laments our focus on serving "various lusts and pleasures" (Titus 3:3); and Peter grieves because of hearts "trained in covetous practices" (2 Pet. 2:12–14, NKJV).

Does this mean we are never to desire pleasure? No. The life of the believer in not a life of negativism but of affirmation and enjoyment. The psalmist said, "Delight yourself in the LORD; and He will give you the desires of your heart" (Ps. 37:4). Again in another Psalm we read, "In Your presence is fullness of joy; in Your right hand there are pleasures forever" (Ps. 16:11). God wants us to immerse ourselves in pleasure by immersing ourselves in Him. God's desires for us are not necessarily contrary to our desires in Him.

Desires that Contest Others
James 4:2

James indicates that while we lust we never are satisfied (4:2a). Consequently, we "commit murder" (4:2). The word for "lust" in verse 2 means "to long for, lust after, covet" and is used with the meaning "to covet evilly" in Acts 20:33.[3] These desires are not just about oneself; instead the focus is obsessively coveting the property of others. James employs a metaphorical sense of murder, which fits well with the tone of the passage.[4] Since the church had the problem of oppressing the poor (cp. Jas. 2:14ff.), they could easily be viewed as "murdering" them. Jesus similarly spoke of metaphorical murder when He indicated we could kill others by our words (Matt. 5:21–22).

When our lusts focus on other people, unhealthy consequences result. First, we experience progressive frustration. "You" and "your" are found in these two verses at least eight times, reminding us our flesh is never satisfied. Satisfaction with what the world offers remains a deceptive mirage. When our minds, bodies, and souls are not yielded to God, life remains one vicious circle of seeking but never becoming satisfied. We "lust" but "do not have" (4:2). The inordinate, misdirected, sinful heart wants what others have. And, when we don't receive it, we lash out in anger and "murder." Sinful pleasure is never able to produce all it promises to the naïve seeker.

Thus, Christians are brought to record lows in their frustrated pursuits. Echoing James (4:2a), John wrote, "Everyone who hates his brother is a murderer; and you know that no murderer has eternal life abiding in him" (1 John 3:15). Covetousness was condemned in God's top ten moral injunctions (Exod. 20:17). "You are envious and you can not obtain" (James 4:2). The term "obtain" literally means "to light upon."[5] Hence, fighting and quarrelling begin to plague the people of God meeting in assembly.

Desires that Conceal Motives
James 4:3

In one sense, James' readers avoided prayer altogether: "You do not have because you do not ask" (4:2). Prayer may be the most presumptuous element of the average Christian's life. But prayer is the resource God gives us not only to obtain His will (cp. 1:5–6) but especially to obtain His will in conquering conflicts. When we can't obtain what we selfishly want, the result is waging war among our members (4:1). Marital conflicts, job discrepancies, national skirmishes, political battles, along with personal inner struggles are all results of unsatisfied personal lusts and envying. If we want the will of God for our lives, all we have to do is ask.

Jesus had much to say about asking in prayer. In the Sermon on the Mount, Christ taught, "Ask, and it will be given to you. . . . For everyone who asks receives" (Matt. 7:7–8; cp. Luke 11:9). Asking implies humility and a consciousness of need.[6] But the asking is never for selfish ends but always for the glory of God. In His sermon Jesus lays down the righteousness, sincerity, humility, purity, and love expected of His followers. He assures them such gifts are theirs if they would only ask through prayer.[7] In addition, Jesus said elsewhere: "Whatever you ask in My name, that will I do, so that the Father may be glorified in the Son. If you ask Me anything in My name, I will do it" (John 14:13–14; also 15:7, 16; 16:23–26). The key to these sayings Jesus makes clear " — so that the Father may be glorified in the Son" (John 14:13).

Thus, James says, "You ask and do not receive, because you ask with wrong motives" (4:3). Rather than God's getting glory through His Son, our motives lock in elsewhere, that is, to "spend it on your pleasures" (4:3). The term "spend" denotes a complete spending with the implication of spending it uselessly and, therefore, wasting the substance.[8] It is the same word used of the prodigal son in Jesus' parable (Luke 15:13–14).

We ask God out of selfish pleasure while pretending to ask for unselfish reasons. How naïve can Christians be who think the God of the Bible does not know our hearts! According to James, a primary reason we don't have our prayers answered is we ask with hypocritical motives. Concealed motives never solve conflict within our hearts or in the public assembly.

Damage from Corrupt Desires
James 4:4–6

James sums up the results of corrupted desires by showing how the church had become friends with the world. He writes: "You adulteresses, do you not know that friendship with the world is hostility toward God? Therefore whoever wishes to be a friend of the world makes himself an enemy of God" (4:4). Christians had metaphorically committed murder (4:2). Now they were spiritual adulterers. James undoubtedly refers to adultery in a spiritual sense of unfaithfulness to God.[9] Jesus also used the term *adulterous* in a figurative sense (cp. Matt. 12:39; 16:4; Mark 8:38). Because James' readers sought after their own selfish desires, they lost their first love for God (Rev. 2:4).

Therefore, they made a spiritually inept "friendship with the world" which turned out to be open "hostility toward God." In short, they were giving to the world the love and devotion that belonged to God and God alone. Imagine it: Christians were more in love with their world than they were with God. But as James makes clear, there is no halfway place one can land. Friends with the world indicated hostility to God. John similarly says, "Do not love the world nor the things in the world. If anyone loves the world, the love of the Father is not in him" (1 John 2:15). Believers possess one allegiance alone—the Lord Jesus Christ.

James now asks if his readers think the Scripture says in vain, "He jealously desires the Spirit which He has made to dwell in us" (4:5). Scholars debate exactly what passage James references since no Old Testament passage exactly concurs with his quotation.[10] Some think it is a loose rendering of Exodus 20:5, while others suppose it's Genesis 6:3–5 or Isaiah 63:8–16, or even a combination of all three. More likely James is not quoting directly from any passage. Rather he is saying the whole tenor of Scripture teaches us that the Holy Spirit who lives within the believer jealously desires to completely possess that believer and control his or her life. The Holy Spirit longs to make us like Jesus and to bring us to a place where no divided loyalties lie. The Spirit of God has but one single desire: namely, to mold us into complete devotion to Jesus Christ. Jesus said of the Spirit, "But when He, the Spirit of truth, comes, He will guide you into all the truth; for He will not speak on His own initiative, but whatever He hears, He will speak; and He will disclose to you what is to come. He will glorify Me, for He will take of Mine and will disclose it to you" (John 16:13–14). Thus, the Spirit of God reveals and glorifies the Lord Jesus in our lives. By revealing Jesus to us and glorifying Him in us, we have the "greater grace" to live humble lives as opposed to selfish, pride-filled pleasures (4:6).

For Memory and Meditation

"You do not have because you do not ask. You ask and do not receive, because you ask with wrong motives, so that you may spend it on your pleasures." James 4:2–3

[1] C. H. Spurgeon, *C. H. Spurgeon's Autobiography, Compiled from His Diary, Letters, and Records, by His Wife and His Private Secretary, 1834–1854*, vol. 1 (Cincinnati: Curts & Jennings, 1898), 189.

[2] Kurt A. Richardson, *James*, vol. 36, The New American Commentary (Nashville: B&H, 1997), 173.

[3] W. E. Vine, Merrill F. Unger, and William White Jr., *Vine's Complete Expository Dictionary of Old and New Testament Words* (Nashville: Thomas Nelson, 1996), 136.

[4] Peter H. Davids, *The Epistle of James: a Commentary on the Greek Text*, New International Greek Testament Commentary (Grand Rapids: Eerdmans, 1982), 159.

[5] Robert L. Thomas, *New American Standard Hebrew-Aramaic and Greek Dictionaries*, updated ed. (Anaheim: Foundation Publications, 1998).

[6] William Hendriksen and Simon J. Kistemaker, *Exposition of the Gospel According to Matthew*, vol. 9, New Testament Commentary (Grand Rapids: Baker Book House, 1953–2001), 361.

[7] D. A. Carson, "Matthew," ed. Frank E. Gaebelein, *The Expositor's Bible Com-*

mentary: Matthew, Mark, Luke (Grand Rapids: Zondervan, 1984), 186.

[8] Johannes P. Louw and Eugene Albert Nida, *Greek-English Lexicon of the New Testament: Based on Semantic Domains* (New York: United Bible Societies, 1996), 574.

[9] Gerhard Kittel, Geoffrey W. Bromiley, and Gerhard Friedrich, eds., *Theological Dictionary of the New Testament* (Grand Rapids: Eerdmans, 1964–), 734.

[10] A. T. Robertson, *Word Pictures in the New Testament* (Nashville: Broadman, 1933).

Living Humbly

Focal Text: James 4:7–12

Humility remains a rare commodity even among Christians. The great British preacher, D. Martyn Lloyd-Jones, insightfully noted, "There is nothing sadder about this present age than the appalling absence of humility; and when this same lack is found in the Church of God, it is the greatest tragedy of all."[1] Jesus often spoke of the obligation His disciples possessed in living humbly before God and others. "Whoever exalts himself shall be humbled; and whoever humbles himself shall be exalted," we hear Him thunder toward the crowds (Matt. 23:12). On another occasion Jesus spoke a parable of two men praying in the temple, one who exalted himself and another who humbled himself. Jesus indicated the one who humbled himself went away from the temple "justified" (Luke 18:9–14).

Humility may be the most confusing virtue in the Christian life. How does one know he or she is humble? Is it possible to work toward humility? Is believing oneself to be humble actually being prideful? James raises several questions about humility in the believer's life in 4:7–12 but not without offering Spirit-inspired answers upon which believers can depend.

Submit and Resist
James 4:7

James begins his lesson on humility by suggesting humility starts with submission to God: "Submit therefore to God. Resist the devil and he will flee from you" (4:7). The term translated "submit" means to place or arrange under.[2] Paul used the term to express all creation being subject to God's authority (Rom. 8:20). All enemies will be put under Christ's feet (1 Cor. 15:25), since Christ "subjects" all things to Himself (Phil. 3:21). The term is also used of the boy Jesus being under the authority of His parents (Luke 2:51), while demons were "subject" to the disciples' power (Luke 10:17, 20).

The first step toward humility, then, is to step toward submission and surrender to God. Submission begins when we recognize God is greater and worthy of more honor than we.[3] The church apparently was fighting among themselves over who deserved more honor (cp. 2:1–7). Is this not reminiscent of the wrangling of the disciples about who would be greatest among them (Luke 9:46; 22:24)? Humility starts with a single step toward surrender to Jesus Christ as Lord.

Surrendering oneself to God, however, will not be taken without response from the underworld. The apostle Peter declared that the devil prowls back and forth upon the earth seeking those whom he can devour (1 Pet. 5:8). Paul warned believers to avoid giving place to the devil (Eph. 4:7) by standing ready to do battle equipped with the whole armor of God (Eph. 6:10–17). Thus, James suggests we must "resist" the devil's assault against us (4:7b). *Resist* means to be "in opposition to," "set oneself against," or "oppose."[4] Any endeavor the Christian pursues for the glory of the cross will always be met with devilish resistance. Hence, we must push back. As a result, hell will "flee" from us. Submitting to God and resisting the devil position the believer on the road to understanding the life of humility.

Come Near and Be Cleansed
James 4:8

Next, James exhorts Christians to approach God and seek the cleansing only He can offer: "Draw near to God and He will draw near to you" (v. 8). The term translated "draw" means to "cause to approach" and therefore to "draw near" or "be at hand" (cp. Matt. 3:2).[5] And the drawing is reciprocal. In other words, if we draw near to God, we're assured God will draw near to us. If the priests in the sanctuary could draw near to God (Exod. 19:22), how much more may the body of Christ draw near to Him (Heb. 7:19)! In fact, Scripture implores us to "draw near with confidence to the throne of grace, so that we may receive mercy and find grace to help in time of need" (Heb. 4:16).

Consequently, James reveals a specific reason believers ought to draw near to His heavenly throne. Similar to the author of Hebrews (Heb. 4:16), James insists drawing near to God will inevitably bring cleansing and purification from sin. He says, "Cleanse your hands, you sinners; and purify your hearts, you double-minded" (4:8). "Cleanse" is a term used for removal of dirt from the outside of a cup (Matt. 25:25). It is also used symbolically as in cleansing one's conscience (Heb. 9:14). Obviously, James is not referring to ceremonial washing of one's hands or even bathing before one eats. Instead James refers to repentance in one's outward conduct. In short, this is a call to clean up one's life. If the believers James addressed wanted to walk closely to God, sin would have to be repudiated.

What is more, James insists, "Purify your hearts" (4:8). He's pointing toward a moral, inward, spiritual purity. The "heart" speaks of the inner life while being "double-minded" indicates divided loyalties. We cannot serve God and anything else (Matt. 6:24). Christ must be first. Surrender to Him. "Blessed are the pure in heart," Jesus said (Matt. 5:8). James reminds believers of our daily necessity to confess our sin.

Be Miserable but Joyful
James 4:9

James further instructs believers not only to "be miserable" but also to "mourn and weep" (4:9). The term translated "miserable" means "to be wretched" and thus to realize one's own misery.[6] James is calling for self-examination. This is a clear call to repentance from sin. Repentance is not a once-for-all act. Instead we are required to live a life of repentance. The apostle Paul summed up the gospel message as "repentance toward God and faith in our Lord Jesus Christ" (Acts 20:21). John said that if we deny we have sin, we are liars and void of the truth. But if we confess our sin (i.e. repent), He is faithful to forgive us and cleanse us from all unrighteousness (1 John 1:8–9).

In addition, James instructs us to "mourn and weep" (4:9). A deeply felt experience, mourning is the same term used of grieving over the loss of a spouse (cp. Rev. 18:7–8). It is also used of regret over the sins of others (2 Cor. 12:21). Weeping is often used in conjunction with mourning. Jesus said those who mourn would experience happiness (Matt. 5:4). James is likely indicating the outcome of those who repent of their sin. The presence of sin in believers' lives brings them to their knees, or so it should! Thus, one's "laughter" would transform into "mourning" while "joy" would reduce to "gloom." Far too many believers today fail to taste the convicting power of the Holy Spirit. James is not calling for what in a former era was dubbed "worm theology." Instead he's calling believers to a thorough examination of the Spirit of God moving within their hearts.

Be Humbled but Exalted
James 4:10

Once God has humbled us in our sin, He fully intends to cleanse us from our sin (cp. Isa. 6:6–7). James says, "Humble yourselves in the presence of the Lord, and He will exalt you" (4:10). Our Lord was fond of saying that whoever exalts oneself will experience humiliation but "whoever humbles himself shall be exalted" (Matt. 23:12; cp. also 18:8; Luke 14:11; 18:14). James appears to recall Jesus' words. The term "humble" is derived from a Greek term indicating an unpretentious aspect in one's behavior.[7] Christ characterized Himself as "gentle and humble" in spirit; thus men and women find rest for their weary souls (Matt. 11:28–29).

And nowhere else must this same type or degree of humility be on display than in the "presence of the Lord" (4:10). While before believers were to humbly receive God's Word (1:21), now they are to humble themselves in His presence. They had believed the words of the prophets and the apostles, but now their actions made James suspicious they didn't believe in the God who provided for them and in whom they should offer their faith and trust. New Testament scholar Kurt Richardson said, "Humbling the self then is not at all a matter of convincing fellow believers of one's own sincerity or contrition"; rather humility toward God is a matter of "relating whole-heartedly to God in recognition of his total claim upon one's life."[8]

Once we genuinely humble ourselves under God's authority, living in humility as a gospel lifestyle, God's promise cannot be mistaken—"He will exalt you" (4:10). Upon first glance this appears like a blatant contradiction. That is, if a person lives in humility, he or she will ultimately live in exaltation. But how can a person live in exaltation if the person is actually living humbly? Nonetheless, the promise of exaltation to those who humble themselves before God is a thread interwoven throughout Scripture (cp. Ps. 139:4; Prov. 3:34; Ezek. 21:26; Matt. 23:12; 1 Pet. 5:6). Even more, when God exalts us, rather than become proud, we are more inclined to give Him glory (1 Cor. 1:31; 2 Cor. 10:17; Jer. 9:24).

Humility Applied
James 4:11–12

In the closing verses of this section, James applies his call for repentance, cleansing, and living in humility to the situation evidently going on in the readers' church. They should not "speak against one another" (4:11) because doing so inevitably reduces to speaking against "the law" and even "judges the law" (v. 11). And James reasons that anyone who pretentiously sets himself or herself up as a judge of the law becomes a judge over it and not under it to do it (v. 11). James discussed earlier the spiritually deficiency of merely *hearing* the Word but not *doing* the Word (1:23–25). There his readers *discounted* the Word; here they are *depreciating* it. In short, by judging the law, they were placing themselves on a par with the Lawgiver—God! Therefore, James responds strongly: "There is only one Lawgiver and Judge, the One who is able to save and to destroy" (4:12). God is the only fit Person to make judgment over others. And His judgment includes the power of life and death, the power "to save and to destroy." Therefore, James ends with a rhetorical question: "Who are you who judge your neighbor?" (v. 12). We would do well to allow James' question to stir within us a similar reaction to what he expected from his original audience. Too often the Christian church stands as judge, jury, and executioner not only of those outside the church but also of those within it. It has been said, "The Christian army is the only army that kills its wounded." If we took James' challenge seriously, the body of Christ would be far less inclined to judge their neighbors and far more inclined to love their neighbors as James indicated in the royal law (2:8).

For Memory and Mediation
"Humble yourselves in the presence of the Lord, and He will exalt you." James 4:10

[1] David Martyn Lloyd-Jones, *Christian Unity: An Exposition of Ephesians 4:1–16* (Grand Rapids: Baker Book House, 1972), 41.

[2] Henry George Liddell, et al., *A Greek-English Lexicon* (Oxford: Clarendon Press, 1996), 1,897.

[3] Thomas D. Lea, *Hebrews, James*, vol. 10, Holman New Testament Commentary (Nashville: B&H, 1999), 321.

[4] William Arndt, Frederick W. Danker, and Walter Bauer, *A Greek-English*

Lexicon of the New Testament and Other Early Christian Literature (Chicago: University of Chicago Press, 2000), 80.

[5] William D. Mounce, *Mounce's Complete Expository Dictionary of Old & New Testament Words* (Grand Rapids: Zondervan, 2006), 1130.

[6] James Strong, *The New Strong's Dictionary of Hebrew and Greek Words* (Nashville: Thomas Nelson, 1996).

[7] Johannes P. Louw and Eugene Albert Nida, *Greek-English Lexicon of the New Testament: Based on Semantic Domains* (New York: United Bible Societies, 1996), 747.

[8] Kurt A. Richardson, *James*, vol. 36, The New American Commentary (Nashville: B&H, 1997), 191.

Leaving God out of Life

Focal Text: James 4:13–17

James Hastings once wrote: "It is the dropping of God out of life that makes life uninteresting; it is the neglect of His presence that shadows our days. . . . The way to find blessedness is to find God; and He is to be found in every ordinary thing in our daily round. We always find Him when we try to do everything for His glory. 'For Thy sake!' This is life's deepest inspiration, and this its highest power."[1]

Apparently dropping God out of daily life had become a pattern for James' readers. As believers, we certainly remain reluctant to consider ourselves independent from God, indifferent toward God, or disrespectful to God. Yet when we ignore coming to Him in prayer, as James' readers obviously did (1:5–6; 4:3), we may rightfully predict a pattern where God drops off life's radar screen. The Lord remains out of the mix. And, even more seriously, believers who leave God out of daily affairs function closer to atheism or deism than biblical Christianity. We might dub them *doctrinal* Christians but *practical* atheists, an oxymoron if ever there was one!

Hence, James 4:13–17 corrects the delusional notion that believers may live joyful, spiritually satisfying lives apart from God's perpetual input. Our future must remain rock-solid in His hands.

Our Proceeding without God
James 4:13

James begins his exhortation with a scenario reminiscent of both Jesus and Old Testament Wisdom literature. Proverbs 27:1 was surely a backdrop to James' concern: "Do not boast about tomorrow, for you do not know what a day may bring forth." Similarly, Jesus told a parable of a rich man who, after becoming wealthy through profitable but selfish business practices, presumed he'd live off his massive fortune the rest of his life. Unfortunately for him, our Lord revealed, "God said to him, 'You fool! This very night your soul is required of you'" (Luke 12:16–21).

Following the precedent of both Scripture and Christ, James writes, "Come now, you who say, 'Today or tomorrow we will go to such and such a city, and spend a year there and engage in business and make a profit.'" The phrase "come now" (cp. 5:1) may be the modern equivalent of "everybody raise your hands" and usually implies both disapproval and a sense of urgency. In essence James says, "OK, everybody raise your hands who makes plans to expand your business and make profits." Note that while James challenges their practice of *proceeding without God*, he in no way faults them for the planning itself. The fact is, we're wise to plan ahead and plan well. However, we must always allow space in our plans with God in mind. At any juncture God might step in and interrupt or even alter the plans. He could even cancel them altogether.

In thinking about planning for the future, several mistakes frequently question the biblical propriety of our plans. First, we choose our own time and schedule without regard to how it might affect others, especially God! Our heavenly Father infallibly knows the beginning and the end. Thus to plan apart from God's timeline not only invites trouble but also mocks the Holy Spirit. A second mistake we often make is choosing a location that only pleases us. How often have pastors set geographical parameters as to where they will and will not serve. If a church is not on the "right side" of town, some shy away from considering the church as a viable ministry opportunity. Third, we mistakenly plan our time limits to stay in a particular place. Fourth, we arrange our activities in life so we alone benefit. For us it's all about *self-interest*. Finally, we mistakenly predict what we are going to get out of our plans and make our plans a reason for boasting about life. As we will see in the text unfolding, each of these presumptions James tackles head-on.

James describes certain believers who concoct a plan to go into a certain city: "Today or tomorrow we will go to such and such a city" (4:13). Thus they begin with a date and a place. It's the picture of a person viewing a map. He locates a certain spot on the map and circles it with a red pen. Then he says to himself, "I'll get a good night's sleep and leave first thing in the morning." Moreover, he has it all worked out precisely how long he'll be there—"spend a year there"—as well as exactly what he'll do—"engage in business." The phrase translated "engage in business" comes from a single Greek word meaning to "be in business" or to "carry on commerce."[2] Interestingly, the word also carries the notion of cheating or exploiting (cp. 2 Pet. 2:3). Whatever the merchant had in mind, he intended to squeeze all the earnings possible within a year's time and move on.

Thus, the presuming businessman doesn't stop to question the result of his well-planned trip. He fully knows his plans will work, and consequently he will "make a profit." What is more, the merchant possessed no interest in the community. He planned investment there for his wife or children. His living arrangements were entirely momentary. He was just passing through. All he sought was personal gain, exploitation driven by self-interest for temporal satisfaction alone. Eternity never entered his mind. God's will remained absent from his thoughts. God dropped out of his life.

While it's good to have goals in business, the Christian's business is the glory of God. "I must be about My Father's business," our Lord insisted (Luke 2:49, NKJV). Believers must glorify God in all their plans as well as in the implementation of those plans.

Our Presuming upon God
James 4:14

James offers no pretense concerning the bottom line of our life: "Yet you do not know what your life will be like tomorrow" (4:14). Knowing the future has been a human obsession since the dawn of time. The writer of Ecclesiastes summed up our general ignorance of the future by using the farmer as a specific example: "Sow your seed in the morning and do not be idle in the evening, for you do not know whether morning or evening sowing will succeed, or whether both of them alike will be good" (Eccl. 11:6; cp. 8:7; 9:12; Ps. 39:6).

Even so, people offer huge amounts of money to

so-called "fortune tellers" to reveal the future. A recent Pew Research report indicated that one in seven Americans overall have consulted a psychic or fortune teller.[3] More troubling is more than one in eight Christians do as well. In addition, while 25 percent of Americans overall believe in astrology (studying the order of the heavenly bodies to predict the future), a whopping 24 percent of professing Christians also believe in astrology! Perhaps James' words are even more relevant today than in the first century.

For all of our obsession with knowing the future, the raw reality is that no one can actually *know* the future (no one, of course, but God). Hence, James informs the gullible merchants of their fundamental ignorance of the future. Then he informs them further of the absence of assurance they'd make it through the night. Some English translations (such as NKJV) pose James' concern in the form of a question. "What is your life?" James inquires before giving his troubling answer to presuming people: "You are just a vapor that appears for a little while and then vanishes away" (4:14). The term "vapor" in the English Bible comes from a Greek term referring to a smoky substance like that of a volcanic eruption or perhaps to steam rising from a cooking pot.[4] It was used by some to symbolize either "nothingness" or to refer to that which quickly passes away. For all the plans the merchants had made, like the foolish rich man who tore down barns and built bigger ones to have enough to "eat, drink and be merry" for a long, pleasure-filled life (Luke 12:16–21), no promise existed that they'd live to enjoy their fortune. Simply put, their life would "vanish." The term translated "vanishes" means "to make unseen," "to hide from sight," or even "to do away with" and remove.[5] Presuming upon God remains a serious breach of trust and makes the creature stand above and independent of his Creator. We cannot presume upon God by ignoring the complexity of life, the uncertainty of life, or the sheer brevity of life. God must never drop out of our plans.

Our Pretentions toward God
James 4:16–17

Laying aside for a moment James' remedy for the person who presumes upon God (4:15), note his description of our pretentions when we leave God out: "But as it is, you boast in your arrogance; all such boasting is evil" (4:16). The Greek term translated "boast" carries the idea expressing an unusually high degree of confidence in someone or something as being exceptionally noteworthy.[6] In this case it is an exceptionally high degree of confidence in oneself. While possessing a healthy self-confidence is in most cases an acceptable practice, James obviously is not referring to healthy self-esteem. Instead he's more in line with the apostle Paul when he wrote: "For through the grace given to me I say to everyone among you not to think more highly of himself than he ought to think; but to think so as to have sound judgment, as God has allotted to each a measure of faith" (Rom. 12:3). The problem with James' readers was that they possessed an overly bloated view of themselves and their abilities to know the future and to make a profit, hardly "sound judgment" or behaving according to an appropriate "measure of faith." Truth be told, the way they were living, they needed no faith at all because they had life all planned out apart from faith! In short, they lived life pretentiously.

And, flowing from a life of pretension inevitably comes a life of sin: "Therefore, to one who knows the right thing to do and does not do it, to him it is sin" (4:17). Paul similarly noted that "whatever is not from faith is sin" (Rom. 14:23). In speaking of a servant who knew his master's bidding but postponed his master's requests, Jesus said: "And that slave who knew his master's will and did not get ready or act in accord with his will, will receive many lashes" (Luke 12:47). While ignorance cannot fully be excused, how much more damaging are the actions of a person who knows that what he or she is doing stands entirely against the will of God? The problem of disconnecting what one does from what one knows is reminiscent of the double-mindedness and inactive faith so embedded within James' audience (cp. 1:22–27; 2:14–26).[7] Only a person who walks with God and depends wholly on God may avoid living the pretentious life.

Our Planning under God
James 4:15

Rewinding back to James' remedy, he insists, "Instead, you ought to say, 'If the Lord wills, we will live and also do this or that'" (4:15). No one lives independently from God. While we may function *as if* we do, sooner or later we'll be confronted with the reality that we could not get away from God. The psalmist confessed in a rhetorical question, "Where can I go from

Your Spirit? Or where can I flee from Your presence?" (Ps. 139:7). He concluded that no place on earth or in heaven could remove him from God's all-seeing eye and pervasive presence (Ps. 139:8–16). Thus the remedy was not running *from* God but running *to* God and running *with* God. *Deo volente* was a phrase first known to be used in 1763. Christians used it as a postscript to indicate "if the Lord wills" or "God willing." James insisted those who heretofore planned without God must change their dishonorable practice into planning with God.

When we think of planning according to God's will, three significant principles come to mind. First, we must have a fundamental willingness to do God's will when we find it. God will not play games with us. If we are unwilling to follow His lead as He reveals it to us, He will know this and simply remain passive in the background. While God is both capable of and willing to intervene at any juncture to accomplish His sovereign purposes, He normally allows us to follow our own path if we choose. The psalmist wrote, "And he gave them their request; but sent leanness into their soul" (106:15, KJV). God will allow us to go astray if we refuse to follow His direction.

Second, God's will is always in harmony with His Word. While everything concerning God's will is not found on the pages of Scripture, we can be sure nothing exists concerning God's will for our lives will ever contradict God's written Word.

Third, knowing God's will takes earnestly seeking Him in prayer. We cannot overemphasize the significance of sincerely asking God in prayer to know His will. Asking God has been a recurrent theme in James (1:5–7; 4:2b–3). Praying and asking were also often found on Jesus' lips (Matt. 7:7, 11; 18:19; 21:22; John 14:13–16; 15:7, 16; 16:23–26). But prayer assumes one does not know the will of God on the one hand and is dependent on God for guidance on the other. James' readers had allowed God to drop out of their lives. We cannot afford to do the same.

For Memory and Meditation
"Therefore, to one who knows the right thing to do and does not do it, to him it is sin." James 4:17

[1] James Hastings, ed., *The Great Texts of the Bible: 1 Corinthians* (New York: T&T Clark, 1912), 313–14.

[2] James Swanson, *Dictionary of Biblical Languages with Semantic Domains: Greek (New Testament)* (Oak Harbor: Logos Research Systems, 1997).

[3] "Many Americans Mix Multiple Faiths" survey, Pew Research Religion and Public Life Project, pewforum.org, 2009.

[4] William Arndt, Frederick W. Danker, and Walter Bauer, *A Greek-English Lexicon of the New Testament and Other Early Christian Literature* (Chicago: University of Chicago Press, 2000), 149.

[5] H. G. Liddell, *A Lexicon: Abridged from Liddell and Scott's Greek-English Lexicon* (Oak Harbor, WA: Logos Research Systems, 1996), 137.

[6] Johannes P. Louw and Eugene Albert Nida, *Greek-English Lexicon of the New Testament: Based on Semantic Domains* (New York: United Bible Societies, 1996), 430.

[7] Kurt A. Richardson, *James*, vol. 36, The New American Commentary (Nashville: B&H, 1997), 202.

God, the Believer, and Money

Focal Text: James 5:1-6

Puritan preacher John Oakes rightly declared, "Few, if any, have been the better for their being rich; but too many have been the worse. What temptations are such daily encountering with, to carnal pleasure and sensuality, to sloth and fleshly ease, to pride and ambition! All which, so far as they are indulged, prove to the detriment of serious religion."[1] How often have men and women—even Christian men and women—been completely corrupted in their desire for the dollar bill.

We nonetheless must be cautiously balanced as we develop James' theme lest we infer wrongly what the inspired author intended concerning money and material things. God's counsel, as we shall see, is not against people who are wealthy *per se*; rather our Lord is concerned with ungodly priorities, ill-tempered greed, and selfish actions of which these particular wealthy people have failed to resist.

Confronting the Wealthy
James 5:1

If we've learned one characteristic about the man James, it's surely his bodacious style. James fears no man. He only fears confusing language. Thus, when he writes, he goes for the jugular, never mincing words though using the most colorful phrases and visionary expressions. James 5:1 exemplifies: "Come now, you rich, weep and howl for your miseries which are coming upon you." The phrase "come now" we discovered

85

in 4:13 usually implies both disapproval and a sense of urgency. The matter cannot wait. James senses confrontation must not delay or it will be too late. The group toward whom James directs his challenge in this section is clear—*you rich*. The term translated "rich" refers to having an abundance of possessions that exceeds normal experience.[2] Thus, it's not just what we call the superrich James addresses; rather it's all those who have an *abundance exceeding the norm*. Hence, James could well be speaking to a large segment of the congregation.

Undoubtedly James based his opening challenge to the church, as he often did in this epistle, on Old Testament Wisdom. Solomon wrote, "The rich rules over the poor, and the borrower becomes the lender's slave" (Prov. 22:7). Recall James' words about the rich hauling the poor into the courts on the one hand (2:6) and now withholding pay on the other (5:4). Again Proverbs observes, "The poor is hated even by his neighbor, but those who love the rich are many" (Prov. 14:20). Moreover, Jesus spoke cautiously about embracing riches: "But woe to you who are rich, for you are receiving your comfort in full" (Luke 6:24).

We must remember, however, that more than just possessing wealth constitutes the church's problem and calls for James' confrontation to the rich and wealthy. The apostle Paul captures the crux in his correspondence to Timothy. "But those who want to get rich fall into temptation and a snare and many foolish and harmful desires which plunge men into ruin and destruction. For the love of money is a root of all sorts of evil, and some by longing for it have wandered away from the faith and pierced themselves with many griefs" (1 Tim. 6:9–10). For Paul, it's those who "want to get rich" who lose their powers of moral resistance and develop "harmful desires" which "plunge men into ruin." The term "plunge" means "to let down," "to bury" or "to be plunged."[3] The picture is drowning (cp. Luke 5:7). Thus, Paul says men's desire for riches drowns them in ruin and disaster.

In addition, Paul makes clear the distinction we've made between possessing wealth and wealth possessing us. Some say money is the root of all evil while others retort that lack of money is the root of all evil. Both Paul and James affirm neither. Rather, as Paul says, the *love* of money is the root. For both apostles, the love of money was a dreadful and dangerous evil. People who once desired the things of God began to crave what wealth could "buy" for them. It's been well said: "Money is the harlot that takes our affections away from God."

Understandably, James calls on the rich to "weep and howl" (5:1) for the miseries they are about to experience. The images solicit from the hearers terror because of God's judgment, which imminently awaits the trumpet blast from heaven. Stewardship focuses in the local church are far from schemes to raise money. Instead God desires to raise people. Through learning to share and give, the rich may best learn God's will for their lives. Proverbs says, "It is the blessing of the LORD that makes rich" (10:22). Thus, God gives.

But He can certainly take away. "For riches are not forever, nor does a crown endure to all generations" (Prov. 27:24). In the final analysis believers, both rich and poor, have a common bond in the Lord Jesus

Christ. Once again, we read, "The rich and the poor have a common bond, the LORD is the maker of them all" (Prov. 22:2).

Determining Actual Worth
James 5:2–3

James now explains what he meant by warning the rich that "miseries" (5:1) awaited them at the first opportunity to strike. He describes their riches as "rotted," "moth-eaten" (v. 2), and "rusted" (5:3)—hardly a positive estimation of their personal portfolios, but from James' point of view an accurate one. In the ancient world three kinds of wealth existed—grain, garments, and gold. James pictures all three kinds of wealth his hearers possessed as corrupted.

First, their riches in grain were "rotted" (5:2). The amount of grain a person possessed in the ancient world indicated the wealth of his estate. Describing the richness God pours out on His covenant people, the psalmist celebrates to highest heaven for the grain God gives: "The meadows are clothed with flocks and the valleys are covered with grain; they shout for joy, yes, they sing" (65:13). Recall that through Joseph's creative ingenuity and managing skills Pharoah became rich beyond compare in the ancient world and his richness was primarily gauged by the grain he stored, grain "beyond measure" (Gen. 41:49). Jesus spoke a parable about a wealthy man whose riches were measured by the number and size of barns he had filled with grain (Luke 12:16–21). And, instead of enjoying his riches, the man's soul was taken from him the very night he had his last barn built. Grain perishes, or in

James' words, becomes "rotted" and therefore worthless.

Second, their riches in garments were "moth-eaten" (5:2b). Another gauge of wealth in the ancient world was the number and quality of garments a person possessed. One of the reasons Joseph was sold by his brothers into Egyptian slavery was jealousy over the fancy coat his father gave him (Gen. 37:3). As a reminder to His people before He brought judgment upon them, God commanded the prophet Ezekiel to rehearse all the blessings He had given to them as His people (Ezek. 16). One of the specific signs of God's generosity was the royal clothing God had given. Ezekiel writes: "I also clothed you with embroidered cloth and put sandals of porpoise skin on your feet; and I wrapped you with fine linen and covered you with silk. . . . Thus you were adorned with gold and silver, and your dress was of fine linen, silk and embroidered cloth. . . . So you were exceedingly beautiful and advanced to royalty" (16:10, 13).

Similarly, James' readers were blessed with the garments of wealth. It's said a change of clothes in the first century meant you were middle-class! Few had more than a single garment to wear. But while God had enriched these Christians, their riches were now in a stage of ruin. Moths invaded their wealthy wardrobes and ruined their prized possessions.

Third, their riches in gold and silver were "rusted" (5:3a). Similar to today, gold was also a standard of wealth in the first century as was silver. However, James' point is that God's judgment will bring about the tarnishing of these precious metals because they assumed gold and silver would last forever.[4]

Jesus Himself warned about the temporal nature of earthly riches like grain, riches, and precious metals. All are subject to unexpected loss. "Do not store up for yourselves treasures on earth, where moth and rust destroy, and where thieves break in and steal" (Matt. 6:19). True riches are kingdom possessions not temporal ones. And kingdom possessions are meant to be funneled not sponged. Believers must be conduits of His blessings, not dead-end streets. Solomon observed, "There is a grievous evil which I have seen under the sun: riches being hoarded by their owner to his hurt" (Eccl. 5:13).

Nor could James' hearers escape, for their corroding riches will stand "a witness against you and will consume your flesh like fire" (5:3). Judgment was sure to come "in the last days." While God blesses the rich now beyond the substance of others, if they are not godly stewards sharing it rather than hoarding it, the riches itself would morph into a mark of God's wrath.

Pressing On to Good Works
James 5:4–6

James now becomes more explicit concerning the nature of the pitiful acts these rich believers committed. "Behold, the pay of the laborers who mowed your fields, and which has been withheld by you, cries out against you" (5:4). Apparently, some of the rich landowners withheld the pay of their hired hands. Unlike a credit-driven culture like ours, which makes it easier for people to exist until the next paycheck, the ancient world knew no such luxury. The average worker was paid daily. Thus, even one day's delay in receiving pay could jeopardize a man's family. The Mosaic law spoke to this matter: "You shall not oppress a hired servant who is poor and needy. . . . You shall give him his wages on his day before the sun sets, for he is poor and sets his heart on it" (Deut. 24:14–15). The rich were so greedy they remained blind to the hurt they caused others by their selfish maneuvers to keep their money.

But they need not think they will escape the all-seeing eye of the Lord since "the outcry of those who did the harvesting has reached the ears of the Lord of Sabaoth" (5:4). Echoing Moses' description of God's people crying out (Deut. 24:15), God hears the cries of the oppressed, and the guilty will not go unpunished. What the rich do in secret and without danger of prosecution will be shouted from the housetops. "Almighty" captures the sense of the Greek here, which has *sabaōth* (transliterated in KJV and NASB), the transliteration of a Hebrew word that means "army."[5]

What is more, the rich appear to be callous toward the oppressed while they pursue their greedy desires. Thus, James indicts them for living "luxuriously on the earth" while leading "a life of wanton pleasure" (5:5). He also indicates they had "fattened" their hearts as in the "day of slaughter" (v. 5). The Greek phrase captured by "lived luxuriously" indicates a life of self-indulgence.[6] For them life was not about pursuing necessities. Rather life revolved around their selfish luxuries. It was all about having what others did not. "Wanton pleasure" similarly means living a self-indulgent way of life especially toward sensual gratification.[7] James piles one descriptive adjective upon another, demonstrating the self-absorbed nature of the lives of the rich. But God never intended it this way. He blessed them with riches in order to assist the poor.

In the end the rich had "condemned and put to death the righteous man" while the righteous man refused to resist the evil committed against him (5:6). Our Lord had commanded, "Whoever takes away your coat, do not withhold your shirt from him either" (Luke 6:29). The rich might have had wealth, but the poor had character. If we matched character with wealth, we could do much good. But matching self-indulgence with wealth only produces sin. Believers must be faithful to use what God gives for the good of others and the glory of their Savior.

For Memory and Meditation

"Whoever hits you on the cheek, offer him the other also; and whoever takes away your coat, do not withhold your shirt from him either." Luke 6:29

[1] James Nichols, *Puritan Sermons*, vol. 3 (Wheaton, IL: Richard Owen Roberts, Publishers, 1981), 411.

[2] William Arndt, Frederick W. Danker, and Walter Bauer, *A Greek-English Lexicon of the New Testament and Other Early Christian Literature* (Chicago: University of Chicago Press, 2000), 831.

[3] Henry George Liddell, et al., *A Greek-English Lexicon* (Oxford: Clarendon Press, 1996), 333.

[4] Kurt A. Richardson, *James*, vol. 36, The New American Commentary (Nashville: B&H, 1997), 206.

[5] Douglas J. Moo, *The Letter of James*, The Pillar New Testament Commentary (Grand Rapids: Eerdmans, 2000), 216.

[6] Arndt, Danker, and Bauer, *A Greek-English Lexicon of the New Testament and Other Early Christian Literature*, 1,018.

[7] Timothy Friberg, Barbara Friberg, and Neva F. Miller, *Analytical Lexicon of the Greek New Testament*, Baker's Greek New Testament Library (Grand Rapids: Baker Books, 2000), 353.

Our Patience, God's Promise

Focal Text: James 5:7–12

The British preacher D. Martyn Lloyd-Jones once confessed, "It is very difficult, as we all know, to be patient with certain people, it is not easy to be longsuffering, and yet if we are to be sanctified, we must take ourselves in hand and develop this part of the Christian character."[1] James exhorts Christian believers to be patient toward fellow comrades in the faith in light of the coming of Christ (5:7a).

We've all experienced mistreatment and misunderstanding which come in a variety of packages. We've all faced intolerable working conditions, conflicts at home, children or relatives taking advantage of us, friends who betray us, and innumerable other painful repercussions. Our natural tendency is to retaliate, returning evil for evil. "They deserve what we give them back," we reason.

James reveals to believers an alternative. Not only does he tell us what we can do in place of revenge, but James also tells us how to do it. He tells us how to do right when we've been wronged.

Be Patient
James 5:7–8a

James begins this section with a simple command to his "brethren," a command stated twice over with an illustration in between: "Therefore be patient, brethren, until the coming of the Lord. The farmer waits for the precious produce. . . . You too be patient" (5:7–8). The term translated "patient," used several times in some form in this passage, means to exhibit internal and external control in difficult circumstances; in short, to be long-suffering or long-tempered[2] (cp. Matt. 18:26, 29; 1 Cor. 13:4; 1 Thess. 5:14; Heb. 6:15). *Patience* expresses nonretaliation. It indicates a person holds his or her spirit in check. Patience is indicative of a Spirit-controlled life.

I heard of an incident that happened on the freeway. A man's car had stalled, and most drivers were taking it fairly well except for one particular guy in a pickup. He laid down on his horn and wouldn't remove his hand. The driver of the stalled car walked back to the driver of the pickup and said, "I'm sorry, but I can't get my car started. If you'll go up there and try, I'll be glad to stay here and blow your horn for you." Needless to say, the man in the pickup ceased blowing his horn.

How often do we lose control of ourselves during the most insignificant circumstances? This indicates a lack of patience. And for James a lack of patience is rooted in a lack of hope. In fact, James frames it in a lack of hope in the coming of the Lord Jesus (5:7).

James will restate his challenge for believers to be patient (5:8a), but not before he offers a practical illustration about what he means concerning patience. The farmer waits patiently for the early and late rains before he expects his crop to produce. The early and late rains indicate the critical role agriculture played in Middle Eastern cultures. Early rains prepared the soil for easy plowing and sowing while the late rains provided the necessary moisture that aided the maturation of cereal grains.[3] The biblical authors were insistent that early and late rains were indicative of God's blessings on His covenant people. The law promised, "He will give the rain for your land in its season, the early and late rain, that you may gather in your grain and your new wine and your oil" (Deut. 11:14). Hence, since God promised sufficient rain for a bountiful harvest, the farmer patiently waited for God to fulfill His obligation. If only believers could be as patient with one another as God is patient with them. Be patient, James reminds his readers.

Be Strong
James 5:8b

In addition to the command to display patience, James insists believers are to be strong. He writes, "Strengthen your hearts, for the coming of the Lord is near" (5:8). The term translated "strengthen" indicates staying in a certain position or direction, and thus to render steadfast, to settle, and/or to confirm.[4] At times the word means to be "fixed" so that something remains unmovable as Jesus indicated concerning the "great gulf fixed" in His parable about the rich man and Lazarus (Luke 16:26). In other contexts the term translated "strengthened" in our present verse means to establish oneself in the truth of the faith once for all handed down to the saints (2 Pet. 1:12; Jude 3). Christians must make their hearts firm; a decisive act is called for. The thought is that of strengthening and supporting in order not to shuffle when things come against you. As one said, "You must put iron in your hearts!"

Similar to James' call to strengthen their hearts is

Paul's statement in his Thessalonian correspondence. However, Paul's context indicates God is the one who strengthens us, making the believer passive in the process (1 Thess. 3:13). What James commands is a firm adherence to the faith in the midst of temptations and trials. Believers must fortify themselves not only for frequent struggles against sin they face but also realize that their struggles are often during the most difficult circumstances.[5] Satan loves to come to us during our most vulnerable moments (Matt. 4:2–3).

In addition, James reveals one of the primary motives believers possess for developing their strong heart convictions, a motive he's mentioned already (5:7)—"the coming of the Lord is near" (5:8). The term "coming" is consistently linked to the second advent of Jesus in the New Testament. The term carries the sense "to come to be present at a particular place—'to come, to arrive, to come to be present.'"[6] Thus, James looks for Jesus' imminent return and calls on believers to also look for Christ to return. The apostle Peter cites the "day of the Lord" coming as a thief (i.e. suddenly and unexpectedly) to inspire Christians concerning "what sort of people ought you to be in holy conduct and godliness" (2 Pet. 3:10–11). Believers, therefore, are to be both patient without and established within because their redemption draws near (cp. Luke 21:28).

Don't Grumble
James 5:9

Next James offers another exhortation to believers in learning how to do right when we've been wronged. He writes, "Do not complain, brethren, against one another, so that you yourselves may not be judged" (5:9). The term translated "complain" rarely occurred outside the New Testament and meant "to sigh or groan with."[7] The idea was that complaining takes place because of oppression or suffering from which the victim desired liberty. Thus, groaning and complaining stemmed from the hope that God would hear and relieve the sufferer's unpleasant circumstances. Often believers who are experiencing the valleys of life look around at other Christians who seem to be sailing without difficulty at all. Consequently, we groan and complain *against them* because they have it easy and we have it rough.

The complaining about which James speaks is the kind that leads to the negative judgment of one another Jesus mentioned in the Sermon on the Mount: "Do not judge so that you will not be judged" (Matt. 7:1). And a key reason Christians were not to judge other Christians was because the Judge was "standing right at the door" (5:9). Indeed James' readers were but a single heartbeat away from the Judge. Death could strike at any moment. Then the grumbler enters the presence of God, who will judge him for every idle word he has spoken.[8]

Endure
James 5:10–11
Before moving on to his fifth and final exhortation to his readers explaining how to act right when others do you wrong, James cites an example of what he means by *endurance*. Believers must learn to endure wrongdoing, and God's prophets in the Old Testament serve as a general reminder of patience during

suffering: "As an example, brethren, of suffering and patience, take the prophets" (5:10). Rejection and subsequent persecution of God's messengers were familiar occurrences in Israel's history. Our Lord denounced the Pharisees as the "sons of those who murdered the prophets" (Matt. 23:31). But James only mentions the prophets in a general way, not naming any individual prophet who patiently suffered (cp. Heb. 11:32–40).

James does mention by name one who endured suffering with patience but not normally referred to as a prophet—*Job* (5:11; the only place in the NT where Job is mentioned). James' readers had heard of Job's perseverance. While Job did not possess the silent suffering we often attach to our understanding of patience, he most certainly did display heroic endurance during his trials. Job endured all Satan threw against him and still maintained his relationship with God.[9] What is more, the outcome of our endurance is recognition of God's mercy and compassion. Are we as patient as Job in the face of persecution enduring to the end? Does our relationship with God weaken during trials, or, like Job, is our relationship with God strengthened through trial?

Don't Swear
James 5:12

James comes to his final exhortation: "But above all, my brethren, do not swear, either by heaven or by earth or with any other oath; but your yes is to be yes, and your no, no, so that you may not fall under judgment" (5:12). The words of the Lord Jesus offer a striking parallel: "But I say to you, make no oath at all [swear not at all, KJV], either by heaven, . . . or by the earth. . . . But let your statement be, 'Yes, yes' or 'No, no'" (Matt. 5:34–35, 37). The Jews avoided using God's name when they swore.[10] And apparently James' readers were guilty of casually using God's name in conversation. Instead of swearing oaths to substantiate one's word, James has a simpler way. Just say yes and no. It's unnecessary to think James includes in his injunction against all oaths those required by legal courts. Some interpret his words in this way. However, as Peter Davids points out, "James, then, prohibits not official oaths, such as in courts . . . but the use of oaths in everyday discourse to prove integrity."[11]

Therefore, contextually James is talking about the practice of indiscriminate oath-taking during times of hostile confrontations. In times of oppression or persecution, one may be tempted to deny his guilt by reinforcing his statement with an oath. For believers it's unnecessary to use meaningless words in order to induce others to believe what we say. Instead we just speak the truth in love.

For Memory and Mediation

"You too be patient; strengthen your hearts, for the coming of the Lord is near." James 5:8

[1] David Martyn Lloyd-Jones, *The Assurance of Our Salvation: Exploring the Depth of Jesus' Prayer for His Own: Studies in John 17* (Wheaton, IL: Crossway Books, 2000), 535.

[2] James Swanson, *Dictionary of Biblical Languages with Semantic Domains: Greek (New Testament)* (Oak Harbor: Logos Research Systems, 1997).

[3] Frank S. Frick, "Rain," ed. David Noel Freedman, *The Anchor Yale Bible Dictionary* (New York: Doubleday, 1992), 612.

[4] William D. Mounce, *Mounce's Complete Expository Dictionary of Old & New*

Testament Words (Grand Rapids: Zondervan, 2006), 1,275.

[5] Douglas J. Moo, *The Letter of James*, The Pillar New Testament Commentary (Grand Rapids: Eerdmans, 2000), 223.

[6] Johannes P. Louw and Eugene Albert Nida, *Greek-English Lexicon of the New Testament: Based on Semantic Domains* (New York: United Bible Societies, 1996), 192–93.

[7] Gerhard Kittel, Gerhard Friedrich, and Geoffrey William Bromiley, eds. *Theological Dictionary of the New Testament* (Grand Rapids: W. B. Eerdmans, 1985), 1,076.

[8] Simon J. Kistemaker and William Hendriksen, *Exposition of James and the Epistles of John*, vol. 14, New Testament Commentary (Grand Rapids: Baker Book House, 1953–2001), 166.

[9] Gary Holloway, *James & Jude,* The College Press NIV Commentary (Joplin, MO: College Press, 1996), James 5:11.

[10] R. C. H. Lenski, *The Interpretation of the Epistle to the Hebrews and of the Epistle of James* (Columbus, OH: Lutheran Book Concern, 1938), 658.

[11] Peter H. Davids, *The Epistle of James: a Commentary on the Greek Text*, New International Greek Testament Commentary (Grand Rapids: Eerdmans, 1982), 190.

100

Prayer: Life's Key to Successful Living

Focal Text: James 5:13–20

Whether life is filled with suffering, sickness, or sin, James addresses the key to living a life pleasing to God in all circumstances—prayer. Griffith Thomas summarized the significance of prayer: "There are many things outside the power of ordinary Christian people . . . but the humblest and least significant Christian can pray, and as 'prayer moves the Hand that moves the world,' perhaps the greatest power we can exert is that which comes through prayer."[1] Similarly, the great Methodist preacher, E. M. Bounds said prayer is the philosopher's stone which transmutes the promises of God into gold.[2]

James understood this truth. The fact is, probably no one in Jerusalem was more qualified to speak on the subject of prayer than James. According to tradition, James carried the nickname "Old Camel Knees" because of thick calluses built up on his knees from years of passionate prayer.[3] One preacher said, "Prayer is the key to unlocking God's prevailing power in your life." For James that key also unlocks the door to successful Christian living, making one's life pleasing to the Lord.

Praying during Difficulty and Delight
James 5:13

James begins this final portion of his letter with a series of questions, the first of which is, "Is anyone among you suffering?" (5:13). James had just given his readers five practical assignments they could do to live pleasingly to the Lord when others had wronged them. Now he tightens the screws down by addressing personal suffering. The word translated "suffering" means to suffer misfortune.[4] James' readers were suffering misfortune, but they chose to complain and even swear. James' immediate answer for those who hurt is to pray: "He must pray" (v. 13). Note that James put his remedy in the form of a necessity. Prayer was not an option. He *must* pray rather than swear (5:12). In addition, the verb form is such that James indicates the Christian must *keep on* praying.[5] The same remedy was spoken on various occasions by our Lord (Matt. 7:7, 11; Mark 11:24; Luke 11:9, 13; John 14:13–16). Moreover, James has already made prayer a significant part of his instruction (1:5–7; 4:2–3).

At least two approaches to unexpected difficulty exist. James mentioned one approach in verse 12—taking oaths and swearing when life gets hard. Here, however, James calls on believers to pray when life gets tough. Consequently, when we fail to follow James' advice, we cut ourselves off from God's prevailing power, and the frequent result is the familiar feeling of being overwhelmed, overcome, beaten down, pushed around, and defeated.

Prayer is James' answer. Prayer is God's answer. The missionary, Jim Elliot, famously said, "The saint who advances on his knees never retreats." It remains almost impossible to overemphasize the role of prayer in the believer's life.

The second question James asks is similar to the first except the circumstances are just the opposite. "Is anyone cheerful? He is to sing praises" (5:13). The term translated "cheerful" means to be of a good mind and attitude.[6] We get words like *enthusiasm* and *enthusiastic* from this Greek word. Proverbs says that while "all the days of the afflicted are bad" the "cheerful heart has a continual feast" (Prov. 15:15). The truth is, many times we are tempted to ignore or neglect God when things are going well for us. Too much easiness in life may spawn an attitude of presumption or independence. "Who needs God when the bank account is full?" we might ask. James says that when our hearts are cheerful and satisfied, we must give praise to our Lord, praise in the form of song. Paul learned to sing praises both in bad times (Acts 16:25) and in good (Phil. 4:10–13).

In addition, observe that praising God is viewed in the same measure of seriousness as praying to God. Praising God in song is actually a form of prayer, and Paul linked musical prayer with the fullness of the Holy Spirit (Eph. 5:18–19). Nowhere does Scripture indicate believers should feel guilty because they are blessed. To feel guilty because one is healthy in the midst of so much disease seems wrongheaded and certainly goes against the grain of biblical truth. We should be able to rejoice when God gives us sound bodies and fit spirits. In periods of suffering and trouble, on the one hand, and bounty and health, on the other, prayerful praise indicates that God's grace is sufficient (cp. 2 Cor. 12:9).

Praying during Sickness and Sin
James 5:14–15

James asks a third question in determining the significant role prayer plays in the believer's life. Up until this time his focus has been on personal prayer. Now James shows the importance of corporate prayer within the body of Christ. He asks, "Is anyone among you sick? Then he must call for the elders of the church and they are to pray over him, anointing him with oil in the name of the Lord; and the prayer offered in faith will restore the one who is sick" (5:14–15). It's one thing to acknowledge one's weakness in privacy before God, and it's another to admit one's troubles to the faith community at large. The term translated "sick" literally means "lacking strength" and is used throughout the New Testament to refer to diseases and infirmities (Matt. 8:17; Acts 9:37; 28:9; John 4:46–47; 11:4).[7]

James instructs the sick person to summon the church "elders" so they may pray over him or her while anointing the person in the Lord's name. "Elders" is a term which bears more than one meaning in the New Testament.[8] *Elder* often refers to an aged person (i.e. *elderly* person) or an older person contrasted with a younger person (cp. 1 Tim. 5:1; Luke 15:25). *Elder* also carries a more formal meaning or positional status within the faith community. For example, members of the Jewish Sanhedrin were called "elders" (Matt. 26:57; Acts 24:1). Being called elder in this sense was more about official role than age.

More importantly for our purposes, "elders" was also used in the early church to refer to leaders in each congregation (Acts 11:30; 14:23; 15:2; 21:18; 1 Tim.

5:17, 19; Titus 1:5; 1 Pet. 5:1; 2 John 1:1; 3 John 1:1; and others). In the New Testament "elder" (Acts 11:30), "bishop" (1 Tim. 3:1), and "pastor" (Eph. 4:11) all point to the same role in the early church. In other words, all elders were bishops, and all bishops were pastors. Interestingly, the term least used in the New Testament to refer to the local church leader(s) is "pastor," the most prominent term we now use. Note also that James uses "elders" (plural) rather than "elder" (singular) indicating, according to some scholars, that a plurality of elders existed in all churches in the New Testament. However, no evidence exists in the New Testament that *requires* all churches to have more than one elder (i.e. pastor). Some churches obviously did have more than a single pastor. Nothing has really changed. Today some churches also have more than one pastor. These churches are usually large churches, and even then one pastor is in charge and is almost always called the senior pastor.

Even so, James is unconcerned here with the number of pastors or elders. Rather his point is that the sick person should take the personal initiative to invite the elder(s) to pray for him or her. Hence, the "prayer offered in faith" will "restore" the sick (5:15). Paul encouraged believers to take care of the sick (1 Thess. 5:14) as did Jesus Himself (Matt. 10:8). The church has an obligation to pray for those who are sick and afflicted. The use of olive oil remained a popular medicine among the ancients. It was used both internally and externally.[9] Jesus attached medicinal value to the use of oil and emphasized prayer in conjunction with anointing (Mark 6:13; Luke 10:34). I might also add that oil was representative both of sanctification and the presence and blessing of God's Spirit (Exod. 40:9; Lev. 7:10; 8:30; 1 Sam. 10:1). Thus, even apart from its medicinal usage, the anointing might have ceremonial significance.

Finally, not only will the prayer in faith restore the sick person physically, but it will also restore him spiritually. James says, "If he has committed sins, they will be forgiven him" (5:15). The term "forgiven" literally meant "to send off" and was richly attested in Greek language from an early period.[10] The person's sins were released and sent away. Sometimes it takes the church of Jesus Christ to assist in helping a person overcome his or her shortcomings. Here the pastor(s) prayed with the failing brother, and God sent His grace. As the apostle Paul insisted, when one member hurts, the whole body hurts (1 Cor. 12:26).

Praying Sincerely and Earnestly
James 5:16–20

James continues the focus on corporate prayer by encouraging prayer to go beyond the scope of calling for elders to pray. Now the whole faith community is exhorted to "confess your sins to one another, and pray for one another so that you may be healed" (5:16). Praying for the sick most certainly is both a duty and a privilege of local church pastors. James corrects the notion, however, that pastors are to be called on exclusively when people are sick physically or spiritually. James speaks to the whole church to "pray for one another." Many Christians would do well to keep this in mind when they are sick and insist that *only if the pastor himself* visits them is the church doing ministry or the pastor doing *his* job. James challenges this fallacious notion.

The term translated "confess" indicates an acceptance of an offer or proposal and thus "to consent."[11] It is a call to agree with and admit without excuse wrongdoing (cp. Matt. 3:6; Mark 1:5). When we confess our sins, we are not making excuses or blaming the other party. Instead we are freely admitting that what we have done is wrong and we sincerely regret our actions. In short, if we had it to do over, we would not act the way we did. Confession is similar to repentance in the New Testament (cp. 1 John 1:9).

James is clear about the outcome of proper prayer: "The effective prayer of a righteous man can accomplish much" (5:16). The word James uses that is translated "effective" denotes "active" or "powerful in action" and is the word from which we get *energy* and its cognates.[12] Some passages translate it "effectual" (cp. 1 Cor. 16:9, KJV). The "much" refers to both the physical healing and the forgiveness of sin.

Elijah can serve as an example for us when it comes to prayer (5:17–18). Why? First because the Jews regarded Elijah as a helper in time of need and one whose coming would pave the way for the Messianic age (Mal. 4:5–6; Mark 9:12; Luke 1:17).[13] Even more, Elijah possessed "a nature like ours." In other words, all believers have access to the kind of "effectual" prayer Elijah displays here. He "prayed earnestly" that it would not rain and prayed just as earnestly that it would (5:18; cp. 1 Kings 18:42). Literally, James says Elijah "prayed with prayer."[14]

One of the most effective tools God gives us to

keep the body of Christ healthy is prayer. In fact, prayer is the means by which God reclaims wayward church members (5:19–20). Through prayer God says many of His people are reunited and reclaimed for His glory. And our reward is great when we turn "a sinner from the error of his way" (5:20). No doubt exists that prayer is God's key to living a successful and pleasing Christian life.

For Memory and Mediation

"Therefore, confess your sins to one another, and pray for one another so that you may be healed. The effective prayer of a righteous man can accomplish much." James 5:16

---

[1] As quoted in Bibliotheca Sacra 136, no. 541 (1979): 59.

[2] Edward M. Bounds, *The Necessity of Prayer* (Oak Harbor, WA: Logos Research Systems, 1999).

[3] Eugene H. Peterson, *The Message: The Bible in Contemporary Language* (Colorado Springs, CO: NavPress, 2005).

[4] William Arndt, Frederick W. Danker, and Walter Bauer, *A Greek-English Lexicon of the New Testament and Other Early Christian Literature* (Chicago: University of Chicago Press, 2000), 500.

[5] A. T. Robertson, *Word Pictures in the New Testament* (Nashville: Broadman, 1933), James 5:13.

[6] Spiros Zodhiates, *The Complete Word Study Dictionary: New Testament* (Chattanooga, TN: AMG Publishers, 2000).

[7] W. E. Vine, Merrill F. Unger, and William White Jr., *Vine's Complete Expository Dictionary of Old and New Testament Words* (Nashville: Thomas Nelson, 1996), 172.

[8] Gerhard Kittel, Gerhard Friedrich, and Geoffrey William Bromiley, eds. *Theological Dictionary of the New Testament* (Grand Rapids: W. B. Eerdmans, 1985), 931.

[9] Robertson, *Word Pictures in the New Testament*, James 5:14.

[10] Kittel, Bromiley, and Friedrich, eds., *Theological Dictionary of the New Testament* (Grand Rapids: Eerdmans, 1964–), 509.

[11] Arndt, Danker, and Bauer, *A Greek-English Lexicon of the New Testament*

and Other Early Christian Literature, 351.

[12] Vine, Unger, and White Jr., *Vine's Complete Expository Dictionary of Old and New Testament Words*, 194.

[13] Douglas J. Moo, *The Letter of James*, The Pillar New Testament Commentary (Grand Rapids: Eerdmans, 2000), 247.

[14] John F. MacArthur Jr., *James*, MacArthur New Testament Commentary (Chicago: Moody Press, 1998), 280.

Appendix

The promises of this book are based on one's relationship to Christ. If you have not yet entered a personal relationship with Jesus Christ, I encourage you to make this wonderful discovery today. I like to use the very simple acrostic—LIFE—to explain this, knowing that God wants you not only to inherit *eternal* life but also to experience *earthly* life to its fullest.

L = Love

It all begins with God's Love. God created you in his image. This means you were created to live in relationship with him. *"For God loved the world in this way: He gave His One and Only Son, so that everyone who believes in Him will Not perish but have eternal life"* (John 3:16).

But if God loves you and desires a relationship with you, why do you feel so isolated from Him?

I = Isolation

This isolation is created by our sin—our rebellion against God—which separates us from him and from others. *"For all have sinned and fall short of the glory of God"* (Romans 3:23). *"For the wages of sin is death, but the gift of God is eternal life in Christ Jesus our Lord"* (Romans 6:23).

You might wonder how you can overcome this isolation and have an intimate relationship with God.

F = Forgiveness

The only solution to man's isolation and separation from a holy God is forgiveness. *"For Christ also suffered for sins once and for all, the righteous for the unrighteous, that He might bring you to God, after being put to death in the fleshly realm but made alive in the spiritual realm"* (1 Peter 3:18).

The only way our relationship can be restored with God is through the forgiveness of our sins. Jesus Christ died on the cross for this very purpose.

E = Eternal Life

You can have a full and abundant life in this present life... and eternal life when you die. *"But to all who did receive Him, He gave them the right to be children of God, to those who believe His name"* (John 1:12). *"A thief comes only to steal and to kill and to destroy. I have come that they may have life and have it in abundance"* (John 10:10).

Is there any reason you wouldn't like to have a personal relationship with God?

THE PLAN OF SALVATION

It's as simple as ABC. All you have to do is:

A = Admit you are a sinner. Turn from your sin and turn to God. *"Repent and turn back, that your sins may be wiped out so that seasons of refreshing may come from the presence of the Lord"* (Acts 3:19).

B = Believe that Jesus died for your sins and rose from the dead enabling you to have life. *"I have written these things to you who believe in the name of the Son of God, so that you may know that you have eternal life"* (1 John 5:13).

C = Confess verbally and publicly your belief in Jesus Christ. *"If you confess with your mouth, 'Jesus is Lord,' and believe in your heart that God raised Him from the dead, you will be saved. With the heart one believes, resulting in righteousness, and with the mouth one confesses, resulting in salvation"* (Rom. 10:9–10).

You can invite Jesus Christ to come into your life right now.

Pray something like this:

"God, I admit that I am a sinner. I believe that you sent Jesus, who died on the cross and rose from the dead, paying the penalty for my sins. I am asking that you forgive me of my sin, and I receive your gift of eternal life. It is in Jesus' name that I ask for this gift. Amen."

Signed _____

Date _____

If you have a friend or family member who is a Christian, tell them about your decision. Then find a church that teaches the Bible, and let them help you go deeper with Christ.

For Teaching Helps
and Additional
Small Group Study
Materials Visit:
Auxanopress.com

Non-Disposable Curriculum

- Study the Bible and build a Christian library!
- Designed for use in any small group.
- Affordable, biblically based, and life oriented.
- Free teaching helps and administrative materials online.
- Choose your own material and stop/start time.

Audio-commentary material for teachers by the author at additional cost.

Other Volumes Available Now

Core Convictions: Confidence About What You Believe
When people have confidence about what they believe, they are more inclined to make daily decisions from a Biblical perspective. Ken Hemphill

Connected Community: Becoming Family Through Church
Only the church can deliver authentic community that will last forever. This study explores the mystery of God's eternal plan to reveal His manifold wisdom through the Church. Ken Hemphill

God's Redemption Story: Old Testament Survey
Explores the story line of the Old Testament by focusing on twelve key events in the life of Israel and linking them together to provide a unified view of God's redemptive work in history. Ken Hemphill

The King and His Community: New Testament Survey
Begins with the birth of Jesus and ends with Him walking among the seven churches of the book of Revelation. It covers key passages that tell the story of the King and the worldwide spread of His church. Kie Bowman

Pray Like It Matters: Intimacy And Power Through Prayer
Prayer makes a difference and it really matters and changes things in our lives as well as others. Our lack of spiritual power is due to our lack of prayer. God will use prayer to shake us and shape us. May He shape each of us into people who genuinely believe that prayer will draw us closer to Him and make us stronger in our faith. Steve Gaines, Ph.D.

Every Spiritual Blessing: A Study Of Ephesians
Ephesians contains some of the richest theology and practical teaching in all of the Bible, it is profound and challenging. As you study Ephesians, I pray you will embrace and express all the scriptual blessings made available to you in Christ. Ken Hemphill